PERSPECTIVES IN

MEXICAN

AMERICAN

STUDIES

Volume 4   1993

Mexican American Studies & Research Center
The University of Arizona
Tucson

EMERGING THEMES

IN MEXICAN AMERICAN RESEARCH

Editor
Juan R. García

Associate Editor
Thomas Gelsinon

TABLE OF CONTENTS

Introduction   vii

Richard Griswold   Chicano Historical Discourse: An
del Castillo   Overview and Evaluation of the 1980s   1

Jorge Hernandez-   The Impact of Seniority
Fujigaki   Principles on the Status of Mexican
                         Steelworkers in the Midwest:
                         Historical Perspectives   26

Devon Peña,   Rural Chicana/o Communities
Rubén Martinez, and   and the Environment: An
Louis McFarland   Attiitudinal Survey of Residents
                         of Costilla County, Colorado   45

Christine Marín   Mexican Americans on the
                         Home Front: Community
                         Organizations in Arizona
                         During World War II   75

Alberto L. Pulido   Mexican American Catholicism
                         in the Southwest: The
                         Transformation of a Popular
                         Religion   93

INTRODUCTION

A major goal of *Perspectives in Mexican American Studies* is to stimulate and promote research into previously unexplored areas, suggest and showcase fresh and various viewpoints and approaches, and present new questions and paradigms that will expand the boundaries of our understanding of Mexican Americans. The works included in Volume 4, "Emerging Themes in Mexican American Research," fulfill that goal.

Chicano and Chicana historical scholarship of the 1980s was more diverse, fragmented, sophisticated, and complex than that produced in the 1960s and 1970s. These characteristics emerged in large part because Chicano/a and non-Chicano/a scholars alike eschewed old paradigms, and explored new themes, issues, and complexities based on class, gender, and generational differences. That is the theme of Richard Griswold del Castillo's "Chicano Historical Discourse in the 1980s: An Overview and Evaluation." In addition to discussing the literature thematically, del Castillo explains how other forces influenced the focus, content, and direction of this research. In the process, he explains why mainstream national publishing houses continue to exclude Mexican Americans from national history textbooks. The essay concludes by positing some hopes, caveats and concerns about the future of Chicano and Chicana scholarship, and a research agenda for the future.

Mexican American scholars produced significant community and regional studies about the Southwest during the 1980s. However, beginning in the mid-1980s, a number of studies about Mexicans and Mexican Americans in the Midwest and Pacific Northwest appeared as part of a new and emerging scholarship. Among the former are Dennis Nodín Valdés', *Al Norte: Agricultural Workers in the Great Lakes Region, 1917-1970;* Zaragosa Vargas', *Proletarians of the North: A History of Mexican Industrial Workers in Detroit and the Midwest, 1913-1933; Forging a Community: The Latino Experience in Northwest Indiana, 1919-1975,* edited by James B. Lane and Edward Escobar; and "Mexicans in the Midwest," the second volume of *Perspectives in Mexican American Studies.* In essence, these studies are also part of the growing literature in regional and community studies.

Mexicans and Mexican Americans traveled to the Midwest as early as 1907 to work in the sugar beet fields, or on railroad maintenance crews. Their numbers increased significantly as a result of the Mexican Revolution of 1910 and the outbreak of World War I in 1914. The war created a severe labor shortage in agriculture, railroads, and industry. Mexicans and Mexican Americans were recruited by agriculturists and industrialists to fill that need. One of the industries in which they made up a significant part of the labor force was the steel industry. In 1919, U.S. Steel recruited African American, Mexican, and Mexican American workers to help break the strike that had crippled the steel industry. Once the strike was over, people of Mexican descent continued to labor in steel. What became of those workers is the focus of Jorge Hernandez-Fujigaki's study, "The Impact of Seniority Principles on the Status of Mexican Steel Workers in the Midwest: Historical Perspectives."

According to Hernandez-Fujigaki, a major turning point for labor in the steel industry was the 1937 agreement between the Steel Workers Organizing Committee and the Carnegie-Illinois subsidiary of U.S. Steel. The main terms in this agreement were the seniority provisions that gave workers basic rights, protections and guarantees. However, by examining personnel records from the mid-1950s, he concludes that these seniority principles served to perpetuate the occupational hierarchy that kept Latinos at the bottom rungs of the industry.

In 1985 California announced plans to build its first giant hazardous waste incinerator in the middle of East Los Angeles, provoking an outcry from the Mexican American and Hispanic residents of that community. To many, this was one more example of how the Hispanic community's environmental and health concerns were being ignored by decision makers. To challenge the decision, a group of Hispanic women called Mothers of East Los Angeles (MELA) battled the state legislature for the next six years. In the end MELA kept both an unwanted prison and the incinerator out of their neighborhood. In 1993, President Bill Clinton's decision to support the North American Free Trade Agreement met with mixed reactions. Initially much of the disagreement centered on its economic implications. Recently, however, the focus has turned to what impact the agreement will have on border cities and the environment.

These two events are examples of the kinds of concerns held by Mexican Americans and other Hispanics. Yet, historically, the views and beliefs of under-represented groups regarding environmental issues have been understudied or neglected. The prevailing belief among mainstream environmentalists, scholars, and decision-makers has been that economic concerns are preponderant in shaping the decisions about environmental issues among ethnic communities. That perception is challenged by Devon Peña, Rubén Martinez, and Louis McFarland in "Rural Chicano Communities and the Environment: An Attitudinal Survey of Residents of Costilla County, Colorado."

The preliminary attitudinal survey they conducted among adults in southern Colorado found that Hispanic residents were very concerned about the impact that mining and exportation of underground water would have on the environment. Residents also favored more ecologically sound economic development strategies for the region. More studies about environmental attitudes of ethnic communities are needed so that their concerns and values are considered in the decision-making process. The present study by Peña, Martinez and McFarland points to one method of measuring these needs, attitudes, and values.

World War II is a watershed in the history of the United States and the world. However, in studying that period, most mainstream historians have overlooked or discounted the contributions and roles of Hispanics. Mexican Americans made great sacrifices in supporting the nation while serving in the armed forces, and on the home front, as well. Not only did Mexican Americans volunteer in unprecedented numbers, they also served valiantly. They emerged from the war as a highly decorated group, and were awarded the greatest number of Medals of Honor.

The war itself had a profound impact on Mexican Americans. It significantly changed the demographics of Mexican American communities. It altered the cultural norms and values of those communities as young people moved away from home, women entered the work force, and individuals left their insulated neighborhoods as part of their military experience. The war also created heightened expectations among Mexican Americans, who believed that their loyalty, courage, and patriotism entitled them to the rights and privileges they had so long struggled for. Unfortunately, prejudice and racism did not disappear during the war. This was evident in the sensationalistic coverage of the Sleepy Lagoon murder trial, and in its aftermath, when the "Zoot Suit Riots" shook Los Angeles in the summer of 1943. Mexican American veterans returning home found themselves barred from restaurants and other public places. Even veterans who had paid the full measure by giving their lives were denied funeral services mainly because they were of Mexican American descent.

Christine Marín's study, "Mexican Americans on the Home Front: Community Organizations in Arizona During World War II," examines some of these issues within the context of Mexican American activities on behalf of the war effort in Tucson, Tempe, Phoenix, and Clifton. It provides insight into the activities of those who were left behind to worry and wonder about the fate of their loved ones as they fought in a foreign war. Her study focuses on how Mexican American communities created their own separate support systems, fought to retain their cultural and ethnic identities, and developed cooperative relationships with Anglos in working toward the common goal of supporting the war effort.

In 1966 a Catholic priest stated: "There is something very basic lacking in the American Catholic Church, which makes it possible for thousands of Spanish Speaking [sic] to leave the Church each year to embrace an alien form of worship. Large numbers of Spanish Speaking Catholics are looking to other religions for something they cannot find in the Catholic religion." Catholic leaders worried that perhaps the Catholic Church had demanded too much of Mexican Americans, and that it had done too little to meet them halfway. In many ways the situation described above was not new or unique. Although Catholicism has been central to the history and culture of Mexicans and Mexican Americans for centuries, there remains a profound misunderstanding of this relationship. In part this is due to the dearth of research in this field.

Alberto L. Pulido describes some of the historical reasons behind the alienation and marginalization of Mexican Americans in the Catholic Church in "Mexican American Catholicism in the Southwest: The Transformation of a Popular Religion." His study examines the impact that the arrival of a European hierarchy had on the popular religion of Mexican Americans in Texas and New Mexico in the second half of the nineteenth century. According to Pulido, the imposition of an institutional or "official" religion by an ethnocentric and insensitive hierarchy on people who embraced and practiced a popular or "non-official religion" had profound consequences. The study is an important beginning in understanding the relationship between the Catholic Church and Hispanics, and providing direction for future research in this field.

All of the articles and essays featured in this volume represent significant departures from what has been the traditional scope of Mexican American research. It is hoped these studies provide other researchers with ideas, directions, and paradigms that they may be able to adopt in expanding our study and knowledge of Mexican Americans in the United States.

My thanks to the authors who contributed their research to this volume. Their cooperation and hard work made our job easier and more rewarding. The continuing support of Macario Saldate, Director of the Mexican American Studies & Research Center, is greatly appreciated. Finally, the publication of *Perspectives* would not be possible without the help of my friend and colleague Tom Gelsinon. His advice, insight, and commitment make working on this series a real pleasure.

Juan R. García
Series Editor
Tucson, Arizona
May 1993

CHICANO HISTORICAL DISCOURSE: AN OVERVIEW AND EVALUATION OF THE 1980s

Richard Griswold del Castillo

T he decade of the 1980s was a period of exceptional vitality in the writing of Chicano/a history, especially in the production of book-length monographs. Chicano/a historians explored new themes and issues, and moved beyond the theoretical concerns of previous decades. Between 1980 and 1990 more than forty books were published in English that contributed to the field of Chicano/a history. Additionally a half dozen or more books on Chicano/a history appeared as Spanish translations in Mexico. The field of Chicano/a history developed so fast that very few had the luxury of reading all that was produced, or of analyzing the parameters of its growth. In an attempt to come to terms with this expanding literature, a number of review essays and short historiographical pieces appeared. But these dealt with only a small sample of this developing discourse.[1]

A review of most of the important books in Chicano/a history published in this decade reveals the development of several areas of interest. Thematically, the literature can be divided into six topical areas that are conceptually overlapping: (1) Community Studies, (2) Regional Surveys, (3) Socio-cultural and Intellectual History, (4) Chicana History, (5) Political History and, (6) U.S.-Mexico-Chicano Relations. In the present article, in addition to reviewing this literature, an analysis of the field is made, as well as suggestions for future research.

The 1980s saw the abandonment of Marxist and internal colonialist paradigms and a movement away from the tendency to focus exclusively on the ways in which Mexicans were victims of Anglo-American economic or social oppression. Most Chicano/a historians embraced a view that examined the complexities of the Mexican American community by analyzing class, generational, and gender concerns. The 1980s saw the slow but steady growth of a Chicana history: a concern with the ways in which Chicanas and *Mexicanas* were actors in dramas that had been overlooked by the male activist historians of the previous decade. Finally, the decade saw a maturation in the field as non-Chicano/a historians began to take an interest in research and writing about Mexican American history. The result was the development of an *historia Chicanesca,* or interpretations of Chicano/a history by non-Chicanos.[2]

The political and social climate of the 1980s influenced historical writing. The Reagan years of conservative rhetoric, cuts in federal programs, and the elaboration of a "me generation" had its echoes among Mexican Americans. Influential Mexican Americans rejected the term "Chicano" and embraced the ideology and terminology of the "decade of the Hispanic." National Hispanic organizations increasingly turned towards a reliance on corporate donations and thus became less independent.[3] The growth of poverty among all Latinos/as contrasted with the growth of a newly prosperous Latino/a middle class. Not only had the socio-economic class structure of Mexican Americans become relatively more diverse, but there was also an increased diversity in the nature of the culture itself as a result of the changing character of immigration from Latin America. Increasingly the older barrios, especially in Southern California (which was the cradle of the Chicano student *movimiento* of the 1970s), became havens for refugees from Central America and Asia.

Thus, Chicano/a history in this decade can be characterized in terms of fragmentation, diversity, and heterogeneity. The complexities of the contemporary age impinged on the ways in which Chicano/a historians interpreted the past. Historians created texts that did not emphasize a political or ideological thesis; in this they were more sophisticated than previous Chicano/a histories.

Community Studies

In the first category, community studies, Chicano/a historians continued a political agenda of the earlier activist era: to contribute to community pride and tell the forgotten story of the contributions of Mexican Americans as part of urban and small town America. Most of all they sought to reaffirm the social and political vitality, as well as the growing demographic importance, of Spanish-speaking communities in the United States. Los Angeles, with the largest urban

Mexican-origin population in the United States, has been the most studied. In the 1980s Chicano/a historians produced a fairly complete history of the Los Angeles barrio in books by Rodolfo Acuña, Francisco Balderrama, Richard Griswold del Castillo, Mauricio Mazón, Antonio Ríos-Bustamante and Pedro Castillo, and Ricardo Romo. These works, along with earlier contributions by Juan Gómez-Quiñones, Albert Camarillo, Abraham Hoffman, and others, present a vivid historical picture of the development of Mexican and Mexican American communities east of the Los Angeles River in the twentieth century.[4] There are still gaps in our knowledge, such as the history of the Los Angeles Mexican American community during the era of the Great Depression and the 1940s. Ironically, what is most lacking is a thorough history of the Chicano movement of the 1960s and 1970s in Los Angeles, including attention to Chicana as well as Chicano contributions to the arts, and relations with other Latino groups that entered the city during that time.

Chicano/a historians of Los Angeles have not yet plumbed the diversity of the city's Spanish-speaking past. Much of the historiography regarding Mexican Americans in Los Angeles tends to overestimate the homogeneity of the Mexicano and Chicano residents. The unstated assumption in most of these histories is that there has been, through the years, an identifiable community of interest among diverse Spanish-speaking groups: the old timers, the new arrivals, the urban migrants and the rural *campesinos*, the women and men, the rich and poor. Well-documented instances of economic and racial oppression are assumed to have forged a unified sense of community. This assumption may be in error in light of the transiency and diversity of the population, which is well-documented. As of 1990, much of the unity of the Los Angeles Mexican American community exists as an idea in the minds of community leaders and intellectuals.

In the 1980s, *Tejano* historians also conducted a search for the historical roots of community. In Texas, community history is dominated by Arnoldo De León. Practically a one-man industry during the 1980s, he produced four books on the history of small towns and cities: Duval, Benavides, San Angelo and Houston. He also wrote, in collaboration with Kenneth Stewart, a survey of the Tejano communities in South Texas during the period before 1900.[5]

De León has done much to document the diversity of life and culture among Texas Mexican Americans. His work should disabuse those who think that a unified Tejano community exits. Speaking of his demographic survey of Tejanos in the nineteenth century, he said, "community was fundamentally diverse in nativity, occupations, family life, education, literacy and urban/rural residence."[6] These differences have led him to hypothesize historical variations in Tejano culture that could be classified according to geographic regions within Texas.

This diversity of experience has been underscored by other Tejano authors writing in the 1980s. Abel Rubio wrote a semi-biographical book studying community land problems in Refugio County during the nineteenth century. Gilberto Miguel Hinojosa wrote a book on Laredo's history up to 1870, and Mario García drafted a lengthy study of El Paso's barrios between 1880 and 1920.[7] In these works there was no consensus regarding the nature of Tejano community. For Rubio, land and oppression was what bound people together; for Hinojosa, the colonial traditions of family figured prominently; and for García, the influence of Mexican immigration was key. As in De León's work, these other Tejano community histories were rich in ethnographic detail about family and daily life. The influence of Anglo American racism on community history became subordinate to the cultural tendencies in Tejano society. Both Hinojosa and García made special efforts to delineate the socio-economic class differences within Tejano communities. Rubio's book ignored this factor and continued with the theme of a Tejano people's struggle against oppression set within the context of his family's history.

Reflecting their contemporary demographic and political importance for Mexican Americans, California and Texas studies dominated community history during the 1980s. There were only a few monographs on barrios outside these two regions. Tom Sheridan wrote an important book on Tucson's Mexican community up to 1941. Sarah Deutsch's regional history of Colorado explored the history of many small *pueblos* from the point of view of women and their families.[8] Sheridan's study highlighted class differentiation within Tucson, while Deutsch emphasized gender differences in social and economic history.

Regional Surveys

One of the main complaints frequently heard from Chicano/a historians is the failure of national publishing houses (almost always located in Boston or New York) to include Mexican Americans in a significant way within their national history text books. Aside from an occasional photograph and mention of César Chávez in high school textbooks, Chicano/a history during the 1980s failed to gain national recognition on par with other national "minority groups." Why was this so?

Rejection letters received by Chicano/a historians from prestigious academic journals often stress that while this ethnic history is interesting or even well done, it lacks a national significance, therefore the author should "try a regional journal." Despite efforts by a few Chicano/a historians, such as Rodolfo Acuña and Mario García, to emphasize the national significance of Mexican American history, the field remained defined as regional in the 1980s.

From the vantage point of textbook editors and Ivy League scholars, the American Southwest (once Mexico's North) is not seen as politically significant as that of the eastern seaboard. The result is that millions of students spend a significant amount of their time reading the local histories of the thirteen English colonies, which are assumed to form the essential core of colonial history of the United States. Meanwhile these students remain completely ignorant of the social, political, and intellectual life of the Spanish-speaking colonies and provinces that later became part of the United States.

One argument that is made to justify this omission is that, up until recently, Mexican Americans were demographically insignificant within the U.S. But this same argument could be made regarding Native Americans (who make up less than one percent of the national population compared to about four percent for Mexican Americans). Nevertheless, much more attention is given in modern U.S. history texts to Native Americans than to Mexican Americans. In the cases of Native and African Americans, I suspect that their history is included (often in a biased and unsatisfactory way from the point of view of African American and Indian scholars) because their history was bound up *from the beginning* with that of the English colonists. The Anglo-Americans did not begin their confrontation with Mexico until well after the American Revolution. Hence, part of the explanation for the relative lack of national attention given to Mexican American history is one of ethnocentrism. Chicano/a history is seen as important only in so far as it is related to the drama of the English-speaking people in the United States. The same is true for Native and African American history, except that their interaction has been more sustained.[9]

All of this is bound up with larger issues of hegemonic discourse and world colonialism so well analyzed recently by Edward Said and before him by Franz Fannon.[10] Given these limitations, it may be impossible to produce a national historical narrative without distortion and stereotyping. For now, a good start would be for a major publisher to commission a U.S. history text co-authored by a Chicano/a, African American, or Native American historian. Even this modest occurence has yet to happen.

During the 1980s Chicano/a historians wrote some very good regional histories and it may be that their quality will demand inclusion in future texts. The most prominent and well-received by a national audience was David Montejano's *Anglos and Mexicans in the Making of Texas, 1836-1986.* This book won several national prizes, including the prestigious Frederick Jackson Turner award of the American Historical Association. Montejano, a sociologist, developed a world systems interpretation of the Mexican-Anglo relationship in Texas. He argued that market forces, more than anything else, shaped race relations in that state. While criticized by some reviewers for focusing too much on Anglo elites and not enough on the actions of the flesh and blood Tejanos who lived the history, the book has won wide recognition for its methodological and theoretical scope.[11]

Another influential regional history was the third edition of Rodolfo Acuña's, *Occupied America,* published by Prentice Hall. Reorganized to follow a more chronological format, this text has been a best seller as an assigned text in the teaching of Chicano/a History classes, especially in California. This edition was notable in its de-emphasis of the internal colonialist argument used in earlier editions. Also important was the attempt to incorporate more of the history of Mexican Americans from the Midwest and Pacific Northwest.[12] The change in subtitles from "Chicano Struggle Toward Liberation" to "A History of Chicanos" indicated a shift of emphasis endemic to the 1980s. Nevertheless, the text retained the critical and even combative tone that had characterized the earlier editions.

Three other surveys published in the 1980s became important supplemental texts in college-level classes. Albert Camarillo's book, *Chicanos in California*, was a workman-like summary of Chicano/a history in the state from 1769 to the present. It also made a special effort to include the history of notable Chicanas. In *Mexicano Resistance in the Southwest,* Robert Rosenbaum produced a history of Mexicano resistance movements in the Southwest during the nineteenth century, with particular attention to New Mexico. Ironically, this book developed confrontationalist themes that were being deemphasized by many Chicano/a historians during the decade. However, his argument that Chicanos/as failed in their resistance movements primarily because they lacked a sense of national identity revised notions about the nature of the Mexican American struggle.[13]

Other regional surveys produced in this era were significant reinterpretations of Spanish colonial histories of Arizona and California. Two major works based on substantial archival labors were James Officer's *Hispanic Arizona* and Douglas Monroy's *Thrown Among Strangers*. Officer's book on Arizona's history during the Spanish and Mexican periods offered a rather pedestrian but scholarly chronicle of the relationship between Arizona's early history and the politics of Sonora. This was the first in-depth survey of this period of Arizona's history since Hubert Howe Bancroft's pioneering work in the 1870s. Douglas Monroy's book, on the other hand, is a literary gem. It is an ambitious attempt to say something new about the well-trod field of California's Spanish and Mexican history (as well as the first few decades of the American period). *Thrown Among Strangers* succeeds with a strong narrative voice, an up-to-date interpretation of current social scientific literature and a kind of deconstruction of archival literature rarely seen in the older scholarship. Monroy tells California's story from the point of view of the Indians, Spanish, Mexicans, and Anglos, and gives attention to issues of gender and class differentiations. Its narrative literary style makes it, in my opinion, one of the best written books in Chicano/a history.[14]

An influential regional survey published in 1982 was David J. Weber's synthesis, *The Mexican Frontier, 1821-1848*. Crisply written with a great deal of careful original research, Weber diagnosed the reasons for Mexico's failure to hold on to its far northern settlements. Among the reasons were problems of distance and administrative weakness at the core (Mexico City) as well as rapacious American traders and hostile Indians. With this book Chicano/a historians were given a much-needed prologue on which to base their own regional studies. As such, this book is a valuable companion to John Fancis Bannon's *The Spanish Borderlands Frontier*.[15]

The only attempt at something like a national history during this period was a survey written by two Anglo American authors, L.H. Gann and Peter J. Duignan. They wanted to chart a history for all the Spanish speaking in the U.S. *Hispanics in the United States* sought to bring together the disparate and diverse histories of Mexican Americans, Puerto Ricans, and Cubans and provide for a discussion of current problems and issues. The title of the book, the conservative political bent of the authors, and the argument of the book, that all "Hispanics" were essentially like other European immigrants in wanting to participate in American material success, insured a negative response from Mexican American readers and reviewers. The main value of the book may have been to spur Chicano/a historians to consider interpreting the history of other Latinos in a more sensitive manner.

Socio-cultural and Intellectual History

The development of a respectable body of work that could be called a Chicano/a history of ideas was a new development in the 1980s that testified to the maturation of the field. There were a number of books that emphasized themes about the ideas and culture of the Mexican people in the United States rather than those of region or community.

Probably one of the best, nominated for a Pulitzer Prize and written with literary accomplishment, was John Chávez's *The Lost Land: The Chicano Image of the Southwest*. Chávez examined the contradictory and ambivalent feelings that Mexican Americans have had about the region they live in, the U.S. Southwest (northern Mexico before 1848). The title of the book referred not only to the American conquest but also to the emotional and intellectual alienation that Mexican Americans have felt and expressed through the years. In *They Called Them Greasers*, Arnoldo De León also explored the idea of alienation, but from the point of view of Anglo-Americans. His was an examination of the elaboration of racist sentiment among Anglo Texans during the nineteenth century, giving stark detail to the ways in which

Anglos constructed a "Tejano Other." We find that for Anglo Texans, the Tejanos were considered ignorant, lazy, dirty, immoral, and treacherous.

The generally high quality of scholarly research and writing in the field of intellectual history continued with the publication of Mauricio Mazón's challenging study of the 1943 "Zoot Suit Riots" in Los Angeles. *Zoot Suit Riots: The Psychology of Symbolic Annihilation* was a complex psycho-social study that gave a radically new interpretation to a well-known event. Mazón's thesis was that the so called "riots" were the result of a breakdown in military discipline, coupled with the projective psychological needs of Anglo American society for a scapegoat.[16] Shaped by his experience as a clinician, Mazón's psycho-history introduced a perspective that gave a new dimension to a deceptively simple event.

The cross fertilization of disciplinary perspectives greatly enhanced Chicano/a history in this decade, and significant historical studies were produced by non-historians, mostly sociologists. This was true of Montejano, as well as for histories written by Mario Barrera, Robert Alvarez, Alfredo Mirandé, and others to be examined in later sections. In the area of cultural and intellectual history, Manuel Peña and Guadalupe San Miguel were non-historians who brought new perspectives to cultural and intellectual history. Peña's *The Texas-Mexican Conjunto: History of a Working Class Music* focused on the social and economic implications of musical expression within an increasingly differentiated Mexican American society. Peña, an anthropologist and musician, explicitly linked the rise of the *conjunto* to a class-specific form of resistance to Americanization and rejection of the more acculturated musical forms embraced by the Mexican American middle class. In *Let Them All Take Heed,* Guadalupe San Miguel, an educator, de-emphasized the class divisions within the Tejano community. His study chronicled the ways that Tejanos fought against discrimination in Texas, embracing new ideas and strategies that departed from pre-World War II assimilationist directions. San Miguel stressed the active role that various Tejano organizations played in opposing segregation and in advancing ideas they believed would improve their children's education.[17]

Another historical study of educational struggle published during the 1980s was *Chicano Education in the Era of Segregation* by Gilbert González. This was a study of the mechanism of educational *de jure* segregation as it developed in American schools after World War I in the Southwest and Southern California. The last half of the book chronicles the desegregation efforts after World War II, especially those leading to the landmark case, *Mendez v. Westminister School District*. González's approach was to look at the economic rationale behind school segregation. He noted how both middle- and working-class Chicano/a organizations united to develop strategies to improve educational opportunities for their children.[18]

During the 1980s Chicano/a historians revised views about the historical role of the Mexican American middle class. Reviled as *tio tacos* or *vendidos* in the 1960s and 1970s, in postmodern America we discovered they were, in reality, the unheralded precursors to the militant 1960s. This new valuation of a hitherto suspect class element within the Chicano/a community coincided with the growth of this same class among Mexican Americans. Mario García's *Mexican Americans: Leadership, Ideology, and Identity, 1930-1960* probed previously untapped archives to assemble a collective biography of influential Mexican Americans who were representative of a "Mexican American Generation." This was a native-born group of men and women who came of age during the decade of the Depression and remained influential up to the start of the Chicano Movement in the 1960s. Valuing patriotism, electoral democracy, formal education and integration, they led important organizations that advanced the civil rights of Mexican Americans during the pre-1960s era. Significantly, they were mostly middle-class men, although some came from the working class, and a number of notable individuals in this group were women.

Another important contribution to the history of ideas as well as to the analysis of the role of socioeconomic class in Chicano/a history was Richard García's study of the Mexican American middle class in San Antonio, Texas, during the period from 1929 to 1941. His analysis of the struggle between the native-born Mexican American elites and the immigrant elites for control of the local culture is an engaging one. He illustrates the fragmentation of a community along the lines of economic class competition as well as nationality. An important contribution to Chicano/a social and intellectual history, García's book analyzes the development of *lo mexicano* as it confronts *lo americano*.[19]

Chicana History

In the 1980s historical studies of gender proliferated in response to a growing Chicana Movement that demanded at first inclusion and then independence from male-centered and dominated history. For the most part, Chicanas wrote their own history, although notable studies done by men about women's history also appeared.

The main direction taken in Chicana history was to "empower" women by interpreting women's historical actions as having efficacy. Sarah Deutsch, for example, in *No Separate Refuge,* probed the ways in which the women of northern New Mexico and southern Colorado changed village life during the period from 1880 to 1940. She saw Hispano women as playing a central role in mediating the cultural consequences brought on by economic changes. In the same manner, Vicki Ruiz, in her book, *Cannery Women, Cannery Lives,* told the stories of forgotten Chicana labor union leaders during the 1930s and made a case for their significant role in organizing unions. She also gave readers an appreciation of the daily work routines and struggles of Chicanas in the packing sheds. In her edited anthology, with Susan Tiano, *Women on the U.S. Mexico Border: Responses to Change,* she brought together collected essays detailing the active role women have played along the international boundary.[20] *Women's Work and Chicano Families* by Patricia Zavella used in-depth case studies, as had Vicki Ruiz, to investigate the lives of Mexican and Chicana cannery workers in California's Santa Clara Valley in a more recent period, the late 1970s. Zavella found that women changed their own lives by establishing work-related networks of support with other women. These networks provided a basis for emotional as well as organizational strength. At the same time, Zavella concluded that basic role expectations for women within the family did not change significantly and led to many conflicts.[21]

Chicana history is still in its infancy as a new area within Chicano/a Studies. Two works published in the 1980s are indicative of what future directions might be taken. Julia Kirk Blackwelder, in her comparative study of Black, White, and Mexican women in San Antonio during the Great Depression, explored the social, political, and cultural dimensions of racial segregation within this Texas city. Using statistical analyses and case studies, Kirk Blackwelder applied a sophisticated methodology to document the primacy of race and caste in social relations between women and the larger society. The comparative frame added tremendously to the authority of her conclusions. Adelaida Del Castillo's edited anthology, *Between Borders: Essays on Mexicana/Chicana History,* was a collection of essays by male and female scholars on a variety of historical subjects: theory, methodology, labor organizing, immigration, education, folklore, patriarchy, and feminism. An additional dimension was the incorporation of various topics on the history of women in Mexico. This book highlighted the diversity and topical scope of Mexicana and Chicana history while serving to stimulate further scholarship in feminist studies.[22]

In the 1980s Ramón Gutiérrez and Richard Griswold del Castillo wrote books that treated issues of concern to Chicanas and their history: sexual politics, class-oriented marriage strategies, gender oppression, and subversion of patriarchy.[23] Both authors used quantitative techniques to find the non-literary expressions of gender relations. The two authors also mined a good deal of primary literature that had been overlooked in previous historical writings. The two works surveyed the main issues in family change and sexual relations among those of Mexican origin from 1500 to the present, Gutiérrez dealing solely with New Mexico.

As recently graduated Chicana Ph.D.'s begin their careers we can expect to have many more monographs and essays published in Chicana history. The historical studies of high quality published in this decade will serve as a model for the 1990s.

Political History

Chicano/a history is, almost by definition, political history in the sense that merely chronicling the existence of a Chicano/a reality within the United States challenges an orthodoxy that considers such activities outside the canon of American historiography. In this category, however, we consider those works that have been explicitly concerned with either evaluating the political activities of the past, or in directly criticizing the historical treatment of Mexicanos and Chicanos by Anglo American institutions. What distinguished Mexican American political history in the more militant 1960s and 1970s continued to be true. The implicit and explicit purpose of these investigations was to act as a guide for future political action. Most of these histories were authored by non-historians, political scientists, and sociologists. Again this can be attributed to the multidisciplinary nature of Chicano/a Studies as taught in the universities, the shortage of trained historians in relation to the vastness of the task, and the richness of the primary sources, whose importance transcends disciplines. In the 1980s individuals who had been intensely involved in the politics of the Chicano Movement began to write their own histories of this period. Their analysis of the immediate past sought to draw lessons for future political activists rather than engage in sterile discussions of theory. In general, Chicano/a political histories attempted to transmit the political lessons of the Chicano Movement to the next generation of activists.

Juan Gómez-Quiñones probably wrote the most comprehensive and suggestive survey of the recent political past. *Chicano Politics: Reality and Promise, 1940-1990,* conceived as one of two volumes by Gómez-Quiñones, presented a sophisticated dissection of the nature of Chicano (called "Mexican") political activity since World War II. He was concerned with nuances of socio-economic class, generation, ideology, national origin, race and identity, as he offered a critique of American Liberalism (called "liberal pluralism") and its perception of Mexican politics. For Gómez-Quiñones, Chicano politics is "an expression of conscious economic and cultural struggle, a conflict of interests engendered by exploitation and conflict stemming from the group oppression under which Mexicans live."[24]

Two other books produced by individuals who had been active in the Chicano Movement were less sweeping in their scope but still written in the same prescriptive and critical tone. *Youth, Identity, and Power: The Chicano Movement* by Carlos Muñoz, Jr., and *United We Win: The Rise and Fall of La Raza Unida Party* by Ignacio M. García had the strengths and shortcomings of participant histories, rich in detail and strong in voice.[25]

Carlos Muñoz, who had been active in the Chicano student movement and La Raza Unida Party, was convinced that historians had ignored the degree to which the activism of the 1960s and 1970s had been due to the power and vitality of the younger generation. He wrote his analysis of the key events and leaders of the Chicano student movement, but not before examining the historical context of political organization from 1930 to 1960. For Muñoz the main theme was one of identity. Whether to be ethnic, working class,

Mexican-oriented, or Americanized has been at the source of many of the student organizational struggles. The Chicano student movement, according to Muñoz, was the first time in Chicano political history that Mexicans in the U.S. sought to base their organization on a working-class, ethnic identity. Muñoz's original contribution was to document and evaluate the past and present tactics and strategies of student leadership.

Ignacio M. García, an organizer with La Raza Unida Party (LRUP) during the 1970s, personally knew many of the leaders who were the main actors in his book. Like Muñoz, he had access to papers and records that an outsider would never have been able to obtain. Also like Muñoz, García was interested in dissecting the successes and ultimate failures of La Raza Unida so that future organizers would "learn from history." The result was an honest appraisal of the problems created by the LRUP's very success. Fearing the gains made by the LRUP, federal and state agencies began a campaign of systematic surveillance and harassment. The LRUP's electoral gains helped open up the system so that Mexican Americans could win elections as candidates in mainstream parties. Their political program co-opted, the LRUP eventually died out as a political entity.

Other institutional or organizational histories also appeared. One written by Carl Allsup sought to narrate the story of the foundation and development of the American G.I. Forum, a Mexican American veterans organization.[26] More of an uncritical paean to the Forum's leadership than a critical study of its controversial political stands on crucial issues, Allsup's book was nonetheless a valuable first step in chronicling this organization's growth.

Julian Samora and Alfredo Mirandé authored a more biting critique of political institutions in their two political histories.[27] Samora and his collaborators advanced a much-needed revision of the history of the Texas Rangers. Using primary sources, including interviews and newspapers, the authors documented the historical evidence pointing to the Rangers' abuse of their authority in dealing with Mexicans and Chicanos. The authors concluded their inquiry by stating that the Rangers had a negative effect on Texas law enforcement. They recommended that the Rangers be abolished, having "indeed outlived their usefulness."[28]

In a similar vein, Alfredo Mirandé investigated the historical record of how Chicanos had been treated by the courts. His thesis was that "since the end of the war between Mexico and the United States, displaced Mexicans, or Chicanos, have been subjected to prejudicial and discriminatory treatment—a double standard of justice that applied one system to Anglo-Americans and another to Chicanos."[29] To support this thesis he marshalled a wealth of historical evidence demonstrating the pervasiveness of the problem. He ended by advancing a theoretical perspective that emphasized a cultural clash of world views rather than the economic or "pathological" explanations of law breaking-activities. Explicitly, *Gringo Justice* called for a new interpretation of Chicano gangs and lawlessness, one that would be rooted in a particular interpretation of the historical Mexican American culture.

One of the most innovative of the political histories to appear during the 1980s was Mario Barrera's *Beyond Aztlán: Ethnic Autonomy in Comparative Perspective*.[30] Barrera argued that the recent history of Mexican American political action had been driven by two conflicting goals: the attempt to preserve community and a drive to achieve equality. His evaluation of the history of the Chicano Movement was that it failed to achieve political success because of the generational and socioeconomic heterogeneity of the Spanish-speaking population and the inherent contradictions bewtween the goals of community and equality. Barrera then offered a comparative study of four countries that have developed political arrangements that accommodate ethnic plurality: Canada, China, Switzerland, and Nicaragua. He concluded that what was needed, in order to prevent the eventual assimilation of Chicanos, was official recognition by the U.S. of multiculturalism. Ultimately this would mean recognition of a degree of regional autonomy for Mexican Americans. Thus with Barrera, historical analysis led to a very concrete political agenda for future action.

U.S.-Mexico/Chicano Relations

One of the most significant changes during the 1980s was the increased awareness on the part of the U. S. government and public of the importance of Mexico. A number of events and trends promoted a wider awareness of the ways in which American fortunes were bound up with Mexico. An energy crisis in the United States in the 1970s led to the promotion of massive loans to Mexico based on its projected oil production. When the price of oil fell in the early 1980s because of conservation and increased production in the U.S., a debt crisis materialized and threatened the U.S. economy. During this decade a much publicized "War on Drugs" led to scandals involving Mexican authorities, and the U.S. pressured the Mexican government to crack down on smugglers. U.S. multinational firms, anxious to compete with Japanese, Korean, and Taiwanese corporations, moved much of their assembly operations to *maquiladoras* located along the U.S.- Mexican border, generating thousands of new jobs and social problems for Mexican *norteños*. Finally, a faltering Mexican economy, produced by the debt crisis, and a prolonged civil war in Central America, supported by U.S. foreign policy, led to greatly increased Mexican and Central American immigration. This in turn led to a long and acrimonious debate over new immigration restrictions to "control our borders," and eventually to the Immigration Reform and Control Act of 1987. All these developments cast Mexican Americans in new roles as interpreters, intermediaries and lobbyists, which the Mexican government explored during the presidencies of Miguel de la Madrid and Carlos Salinas de Gotari. Mexican analysts soon learned that Chicano/a activists had been adovocating ideas that supported Mexican cultural and political interests.

After all, Chicano/a activists had been talking about *Aztlán* as an extension of Mexico and of a binational community *sin fronteras.* They offered an in-house critique of American treatment of Mexicans in the U.S. and sought to counter racist attacks against Mexican culture. Academically, Chicanos/as became increasingly involved during the 1980s in conferences and activities with Mexican intellectuals and activists. During the same period, Chicano/a academics became more interested in international exchanges with Mexico, Latin America, and even Europe.

Against this background it should be no surprise that Chicano/a historians took a new interest in the Mexican connection, and, at the same time, that Mexican intellectuals began to notice the work of their American cousins. There have been, of course, many points of convergence between major events in Mexican historiography and Chicano/a history, the main ones being the Mexican War and the Treaty of Guadalupe Hidalgo, the Mexican Revolution and its relationship to Mexicans in the borderlands, and the social, economic, and political consequences of more than one hundred years of Mexican immigration to the United States. Chicano/a scholars have been aware of these points of convergence for many years and have often gone to Mexican primary sources to gather the evidence needed for their histories. There has also grown up a small but important group of Mexican scholars who wrote on historical themes dealing with Mexican Americans during the 1970s and 1980s.[31]

In Mexico, a number of historical anthologies and translations of works written by Chicano/a scholars appeared. Siglo Veintiuno, a major Mexican publishing house, brought out two volumes on Chicano labor history authored by Juan Gómez-Quiñones and David Maciel.[32] Published in Spanish, these two volumes joined a small and growing body of Chicano/a history that was available to Mexican audiences. The first volume, by Gómez-Quiñones, was a study of Chicano labor history in the Mexican frontier up to 1848. He argued that, despite regional differences, the Mexican working class, on both sides of the border, was unified by commonalities of culture, belief, work routines, family life, and economic organization. The second volume, by David Maciel, traced the history of Mexicano and Chicano labor organizing activities in the United States, presenting evidence of Mexican influences on U.S. labor movements. Another important translation was of David J. Weber's book, *The Mexican Frontier*, by the Fondo de Cultura Económica in 1988. This enabled a larger audience to read about the latest synthesis of the Mexican period as seen from the perspective of the United States.[33]

The border has naturally been the focus of attention for Chicano/a historians as well. Three books in the 1980s highlighted the historical importance of this region. Oscar Martínez's *Troublesome Border*, besides being a history of the complex ethnic, regional, and international transformations in this region, called for a rethinking of the border by U.S. and Mexican policy makers. In his words, "Demographically, economically, linguistically, and culturally the U.S. border area is functionally an extension of Mexico, and in a similar fashion, the Mexican border zone is an extension of economic, social, and cultural influences from the United States. . .Recognition of the overlap concept necessitates putting aside nationalistic considerations that cause people to see the border as an untouchable impenetrable barrier."[34] Another book, *The Treaty of Guadalupe Hidalgo*, also looked at the social, legal, economic, and political consequences of the establishment of the border in 1848.[35]   This study sought to examine the impact of this treaty on the Mexican and U.S. historical consciousness, and to establish the present-day importance of this international agreement. The end result was to demonstrate a commonality of historical interest between Mexicans and Chicanos centered on interpretations of the meaning of this document, and ultimately about the U.S.-Mexican relationship. Finally, Juan Ramón García wrote a history of the U.S. efforts to deport and repatriate a million Mexican immigrants in "Operation Wetback" in 1954.[36] This study relied heavily on research in Mexican archival sources and analyzed the moral dilemma that the Mexican government experienced during this event. García found that Chicano leaders were by no means unified in their opposition to this policy and that many Texas growers were perhaps militantly anti-INS. As a study, this book presented us with a more complicated and less Manichean view of "Operation Wetback" as seen from both sides of the border.

Francisco Balderrama, Robert Alvarez, and Abraham Hoffman wrote histories about the relations between Mexican and Chicano communities in the United States.[37] Balderrama investigated the activities of the Mexican Consulate in Los Angeles during the 1930s, when the Mexican consul attempted to support the Mexican-born, who were struggling to make a living while retaining their culture. This book indicated something of the historical viability of the link between the Chicano community, Mexican immigrants, and Mexican governmental representatives. Alvarez researched the historical roots of the Mexican settlers in Lemon Grove, California, by examining the family histories of generations of Baja Californians. He disclosed how the ties between Mexican and U.S. families were maintained by means of *parentesco* (family liniage), *confianza* (trust), and *compadrazgo* (godparents). This was a history showing how binational families were an integral part of one Chicano community. Hoffman studied the social and political consequences of the murder of two Mexican youths from prominent Mexican families during the Depression. He skillfully recreated the tragic circumstances surrounding the killings that took place in Oklahoma in 1931, while offering a subtle critique of American racial and judicial prejudice.

Conclusions

This review of some of the major monographs and book surveys published during the decade of the 1980s is incomplete, since I have not dealt with an even larger body of work represented by historical anthologies, essays, and articles. Nevertheless, it provides a basis for evaluating the current (as of 1990) status of Chicano/a history and suggests a likely agenda for future growth in the field.

During the 1980s the character of discourse in Chicano/a history diversified and became more complex. Non-Chicanos began contributing their interpretations of the Mexican American past. Chicanas raised issues related to gender, apart from the older debate over the political economy and racism. Non-historians offered their explanations of the past using their theoretical and methodological skills, and some historians began to see Chicano/a history in comparative and international dimensions.

There were continuities with the past in that a debate continued between those who stressed working-class conflict and confrontation as a major interpretive theme, and those who stressed the importance of accommodation, adjustment, and internal diversity. These two "schools," representing the conflictive and pluralist views of Chicano/a history, continued their debate with representative histories by Rodolfo Acuña (conflict) and Mario García (pluralist) appearing in the decade. Most of the political histories were of the conflict mode of analysis, while most of the community, social, and intellectual studies tended toward the pluralist approach.

A whole range of "other" interpretations have emerged to blur these lines of debate. Historians such as De León, Ruiz, Martínez, and Deutsch evaluated both conflict and accommodation as equally important themes in Chicano/a history. Others such as Mazón and Monroy saw conflict as a surface manifestation of deeper psychological and cultural forces. Indeed, the tendency toward conceptualizing Chicano/a history in terms of gender, class, and generational differentiation seemed to internalize the idea of conflict. We might expect that, in the future, Chicano/a historians will see more differentiation and internal strife than previously.

While there has been a burst of creativity in the historical study of Chicanos/as during this decade, there is no assurance that it will continue into the 1990s. One of the most troubling facts about the

1980s and the present is the relatively small number of Chicanos/as who are entering Ph.D. programs in History as compared to the numbers who did so during the 1960s and 1970s. In the 1990s we cannot expect a great deal of new talent to emerge. There will be promising new work by Latinas and Chicanas, many of whom are just now beginning their careers. And, we can expect a gender-based critique of an older male-centered Chicano history. But unless the older generation of Chicano/a historians continue to be as creative as they were in their younger years (is there a point of diminishing returns?) we may expect to see a maturation of perspectives, perhaps an inevitable drift towards more conservative attitudes. Elsewhere, in evaluating California Chicano/a history, I have argued that this already has taken place. However, that pessimistic view may not be warranted, given the larger picture.

What would be a viable agenda for future progress in the field? First and foremost, more attention needs to be given to encouraging Latinos/as and Chicanos/as to major in History and pursue graduate degrees. To do this we need to have more tenured professors in history departments acting as mentors and role models. To encourage this process and to act as a clearing house of information for scholarships, fellowships, career opportunities and the like, we need a discipline-specific organization. The National Association for Chicano Studies (NACS) has long recognized and spoken out against the systematic problems inherent in all disciplines, but a special effort needs to be made to draw together Chicano/a historians as a caucus within NACS or as a separate organization. This organization would give increased visibility and prominence to Chicano/a History as a field within Chicano/a Studies.

Another item for the future would be to work toward re-establishing an academic journal that would provide publishing opportunities for Chicano/a historians. Many years ago *The Journal of Mexican American History* had a quixotic and brief life, and, of course there have been a number of Chicano journals that have published history over the years. But they have all disappeared. The sole survivor in terms of a nationally recognized multidisciplinary Chicano/a Studies journal is *Aztlán,* published out of UCLA. A journal devoted to Chicano/a and Latino/a History would greatly invigorate and stimulate new talent. The economics and organizational difficulties of such an endeavor are obvious. Such a journal would almost certainly have to be subsidized by a major research university and it would take the commitment of a senior Chicano/a historian over a number of years to make it a success. Finally, the demographic changes of the past decade are going to demand that Chicano/a historians broaden their conceptualization of the Chicano/a community and Chicano/a history. Here I am thinking of the millions of Spanish-speaking, non-Mexican residents of the United States who have been euphemistically and controversially lumped together under the label "Hispanic." The tendency in recent years for Chicanos/as to embrace the label "Latino" is only one symptom of a profound shift in orientation towards a more pan-Latin approach to Chicano/a Studies. I fully expect to see a number of comparative survey histories authored by Chicanos/as and other Latinos/as, as attempts are made to conceptualize a larger Latino history. The Puerto Rican, Cuban, Dominican, Salvadoran, Guatamalan, and Panamanian origin populations in the United States are growing and will demand a historical presence. Just how their communities will be interpreted in the light of the Chicano/a histo-riography remains an open question to be answered during the 1990s.

NOTES

[1] For reasons of practicality, this essay will focus mostly on the historical mono-graphs and books published in the 1980s. Earlier historiographic essays written during this decade are as follows: Alex Saragoza, "Ideological Distortions in Recent Chicano Historiography: The Internal Model and Chicano Historiographical Interpretation," *Aztlán: A Journal of Chicano Studies,* Vol. 18, no. 1 (Spring 1987): 7-28; "Recent Chicano Historiography: An Interpretive Essay," *Aztlán: A Journal of Chicano Studies,* Vol. 19, no. 1 (1988-1990): 1-78; David Gutierrez, "The Third Generation: Recent Trends in Chicano/Mexican American Historiography," *Mexican Studies/Estudios Mexicanos,* Vol. 5, no. 1 (Summer 1989): 281-296; Rodolfo Acuña, "The Struggles of Class and Gender: Current Research in Chicano Studies," *Journal of Ethnic Studies,* (Spring 1990): 135-138; Vicki Ruiz, "Texture, Text, and Context: New Approaches in Chicano Historiography," *Mexican Studies/Estudios Mexicanos,* Vol. 2, no. 1 (Winter 1986): 145-152; Richard Griswold del Castillo, "New Perspectives on the Mexican and American Borderlands," *Latin American Research Review,* Vol. 19, no. 1 (1984): 199-209; "Tejanos and California Chicanos: Regional Variations in Mexican American History," *Mexican Studies/Estudios Mexicanos,* Vol. 1, no.1 (Winter 1985): 134-139; "Southern California Chicano History: Regional Origins and a National Critique," *Aztlán: A Journal of Chicano*

Studies, Vol. 19, no. 1 (1988-1990): 109-124; Abraham Hoffman, "The Writing of Chicano Urban History: From Bare Beginnings to Significant Studies," *Journal of Urban History*, Vol 12, no. 2 (February 1986): 199-205; Arnoldo De León, "Texas Mexicans: Twentieth Century Interpretations," in *Texas Through Time: Evolving Interpretations*, Walter Buenger and Robert A. Calvert, eds. (College Station: Texas A & M University Press, 1990); John R. Chávez, "Rubio's *Stolen Heritage* in Tejano Historiography," unpublished manuscript presented at National Association for Chicano Studies, March 4, 1988. For a comprehensive review of the historical literature up to 1974 see Juan Gómez-Quiñones and Luis Arroyo, "On the State of Chicano History: Observations on its Development, Interpretation and Theory, 1970-1974," *Western Historical Quarterly* 11, no. 3 (July 1980): 307-322.

[2] The term "Chicanesca" is one used by literary critics to describe the kind of literature written by non-Chicanos about Chicano topics. It does not necessarily have a pejorative connotation.

[3] See Isidro Ortiz," Reaganomics and Latino Organizational Strategies," *Ethnic and Gender Boundaries in the United States: Studies of Asian, Black, Mexican and Native Americans*, Sucheng Chan, ed. (New York: Edwin Mellen Press, 1989).

[4] Rodolfo Acuña, *Community Under Siege: A Chronicle of Chicanos East of the Los Angeles River, 1945-1975* (Los Angeles: Chicano Studies Research Center, 1984); Ricardo Romo, *East Los Angeles: History of a Barrio* (Austin: University of Texas Press, 1983); Richard Griswold del Castillo, *The Los Angeles Barrio 1850-1890: A Social History* (Berkeley and Los Angeles: University of California Press, 1980); Francisco Balderrama, *In Defense of La Raza: The Los Angeles Mexican Consulate and the Mexican Community, 1929-1936* (Tucson: University of Arizona Press, 1983); Antonio Ríos-Bustamante and Pedro Castillo, *An Illustrated History of Mexican Los Angeles, 1781-1985* (Los Angeles: Chicano Studies Research Center, 1986); Mauricio Mazón, *The Zoot Suit Riots: The Psychology of Symbolic Annihilation* (Austin: University of Texas Press, 1984); Carlos Muñoz, Jr., *Youth, Identity, and Power: The Chicano Movement* (London and New York: Verso Press, 1989). Historical works on the Los Angeles barrio published before 1980 were Juan Gómez-Quiñones, *Sembradores: Ricardo Flores Magón y el Partido Liberal Mexicano: A Eulogy and Critique* (Los Angeles: Chicano Studies Research Center, 1973); Albert Camarillo, *Chicanos in a Changing Society: From Mexican Pueblos to American Barrios in Santa Barbara and Southern California, 1848-1930* (Cambridge: Harvard University Press, 1979); Abraham Hoffman, *Unwanted Mexican Americans in the Great Depression: Repatriation Pressures, 1929-1939* (Tucson: University of Arizona Press, 1974).

[5] De León has been unquestionably the most prolific Chicano historian of the 1980s. The books listed below are not a complete listing of his output during this period, since his other works were outside the category of community history. See his *Benavides: The Town and Its Founder* (Benavides, Texas: Benavides Centennial Committee, 1980); *A Social History of Duval County* (San Diego, Texas: County Commissioners' Court, 1978); *Las Fiestas Patrias: Biographic Notes on the Chicano Presence in San Angelo, Texas* (San Antonio: Caravel Press, 1978); and *Ethnicity in the Sunbelt: Mexican Americans in Houston, Texas* (Houston: Mexican American Studies Center, 1989). His survey of Tejano community history appears in two

books, *The Tejano Community, 1836-1900* (Albuquerque: University of New Mexico Press, 1982) and *Tejanos and the Numbers Game* (Albuquerque: University of New Mexico Press, 1989).

[6] Arnoldo De León, "Texas-Mexicans: Marginal Folks or Historical Insiders," Unpublished manuscript.

[7] Abel Rubio, *Stolen Heritage: A Mexican American's Rediscovery of His Family's Lost Land Grant* (Austin: Eakin, Press, 1986); Gilberto Miguel Hinojosa, *A Borderlands Town in Transition: Laredo, 1755-1870* (College Station: Texas A & M Press, 1983); Mario T. García, *Desert Immigrants: The Mexicans of El Paso, 1880-1920* (London and New Haven: Yale University Press, 1980).

[8] Thomas E. Sheridan, *Los Tucsonenses: The Mexican Community in Tucson, 1854-1941* (Tucson: University of Arizona Press, 1986); Sarah Deutsch, *No Separate Refuge: Culture, Class and Gender on the Anglo-Hispanic Frontier in the American Southwest, 1880-1940.*

[9] All U.S. History texts have a section dealing with the Mexican War and it is in this section that students first learn about the Mexicans living in the present-day U.S. After 1848, however they disappear, perhaps to reemerge in the 1960s marching in Farm Worker demonstrations. The same kind of disappearance occurs with regard to Native American and, to a lesser extent, African Americans. The best current college-level text that has been praised for attempting national inclusion of Mexican Americans is Nash, Jeffery et. al., *The American People: Creating a Nation and a Society* (New York: Harper & Row, 1986). But the secondary school version of this text has significant flaws of omission.

[10] Edward Said, *Orientalism* (New York: Pantheon Books, 1978); Franz Fannon, *The Wretched of the Earth* (New York: Grove Press, 1963).

[11] David Montejano, *Anglos and Mexicans in the Making of Texas, 1836-1986* (Austin: University of Texas Press, 1987). See reviews by Mario T. García in *The American Historical Review,* Vol. 94, no. 3, (June 1989): 1184-5 and by Tomás E. Chávez in *The Journal of American History,* Vol. 73, no. 3 (December 1988): 993-994.

[12] Rodoflo Acuña, *Occupied America: A History of Chicanos,* Third ed. (New York: Prentice Hall, 1987).

[13] Robert J. Rosenbaum, *Mexicano Resistance in the Southwest: "The Sacred Right of Self Preservation"* (Austin: University of Texas Press, 1981). This was a revision of earlier Hobsbawmian analyses such as those included in Pedro Castillo's and Alberto Camarillo's (eds.) *Furia y Muerte: Los Bandidos Chicanos,* Chicano Studies Research Center, Monograph No. 4 (Los Angeles: Aztlán Publications, 1973).

[14] James Officer, *Hispanic Arizona, 1536-1856* (Tucson: University of Arizona Press, 1987); Douglas Monroy, *Thrown Among Strangers: The Making of Mexican Culture in Frontier California* (Berkeley and Los Angeles: University of California Press, 1990).

[15] David Weber, *The Mexican Frontier, 1821-1846: The American Southwest Under Mexico* (Albuquerque: University of New Mexico Press, 1982); John Francis Bannon, *The Spanish Borderlands Frontier, 1513-1821* (New York: Holt, Rinehart and Winston, Inc., 1963). David Weber published a new interpretation of the

Spanish borderlands in *The Spanish Frontier in North America* (New Haven and Yale: Yale University Press, 1992).

[16] Mauricio Mazón, *The Zoot Suit Riots: The Psychology of Symbolic Annihilation* (Austin: University of Texas Press, 1984).

[17] Manuel Peña, *The Texas Mexican Conjunto: A History of Working-Class Music* (Austin: University of Texas Press, 1985); Guadalupe San Miguel Jr., *"Let All of Them Take Heed": Mexican Americans and the Campaign for Educational Equality in Texas, 1910-1981* (Austin: University of Texas Press, 1987). Both books are compared and reviewed by David Gutierrez in "The Third Generation: Reflections on Recent Chicano Historiography," *Mexican Studies,* Vol. 5, no. 2 (Summer 1989): 281-297.

[18] Gilbert Gonzalez, *Chicano Education in the Era of Segregation* (Philadelphia: The Balch Institute Press, 1990).

[19] Richard A. García, *Rise of the Mexican American Middle Class: San Antonio, 1929-1941* (College Station: Texas A & M Press, 1991).

[20] Vicki Ruiz and Susan Tiano (eds.) *Home on the U.S.-Mexico Border: Responses to Change* (Boulder, Colorado: Westview Press, 1987.

[21] Sarah Deutsch, *No Separate Refuge: Culture, Class and Gender on the Anglo-Hispanic Frontier in the American Southwest, 1880-1940* (New York: Oxford University Press, 1987); Vicki L. Ruiz, *Cannery Women: Cannery Lives: Mexican Women, Unionization, and the California Food Processing Industry, 1930-1950* (Albuquerque: University of New Mexico Press, 1987); Patricia Zavella, *Women's Work and Chicano Families: Cannery Workers of Santa Clara Valley* (New York: Cornell University Press, 1987).

[22] Julia Kirk Blackwelder, *Women of the Depression: Caste and Culture in San Antonio, 1929-1939* (College Station: Texas A & M Press, 1984); Adelaida Del Castillo (ed.), *Between Borders: Essays on Mexicana/Chicana History* (Encino: Floricanto Press, 1990).

[23] Ramón Gutierrez, *When Jesus Came, The Corn Mothers Went Away: Marriage, Sexuality, and Power in New Mexico, 1500-1846* (Palo Alto: Stanford University Press, 1990); Richard Griswold del Castillo, *La Familia: Chicano Families in the Urban Southwest, 1848 to the Present* (Notre Dame: University of Notre Dame Press, 1984).

[24] Juan Gómez-Quiñones, *Chicano Politics: Reality and Promise, 1940-1990* (Albuquerque: University of New Mexico Press, 1990), p. 28.

[25] Carlos Muñoz, Jr., *Youth, Identity, and Power: The Chicano Movement* (London and New York: Verso Press, 1989); Ignacio M. García, *United We Win: The Rise and Fall of La Raza Unida Party* (Tucson: Mexican American Studies & Research Center, 1989).

[26] Carl Allsup, *The American G. I. Forum: Origins and Evolution* (Austin: Center for Mexican American Studies, University of Texas Press, 1982).

[27] Alfredo Mirandé, *Gringo Justice* (Notre Dame: University of Notre Dame Press, 1987); Julian Samora, Joe Bernal, Albert Peña, *Gunpowder Justice: A Reassessment of the Texas Rangers* (Notre Dame: University of Notre Dame Press, 1979).

[28] Samora, et al., p. 166-167.

[29] Mirandé, p. ix.

[30] Mario Barrera, *Beyond Aztlán: Ethnic Autonomy in Comparative Perspective* (New York, Westport, Connecticut and London: Praeger, 1988).

[31] Some of the more important historical works written by Mexicanos are Mercedes Carreras de Velasco, *Los mexicanos que devolvio la crises, 1929-1932* (Mexico, D.F.: Secretaría de Relaciones Exteriores, 1974); Arturo Santamaría Gómez, *La izquierda norteamericana y los trabajadores indocumentados* (Mexico, D.F.: Ediciones de Cultura Popular, UNAM, 1988); Remedios Gómez Arnau, *Mexico y la protección de sus nacionales en los Estados Unidos* (Mexico D.F: Centro de Investigación Sobre los Estados Unidos de America, 1990); Saul Fernando Alanis Enciso, *La primera gran repatriación: los mexicanos en Estados Unidos y el gobierno de México (1918-1922)* Mexico D.F., tesis, Facultad de Filosofía y Letras, UNAM 1987; Gilberto López y Rivas, *Chicano, o la explotación de "La Raza"* (Mexico D.F.: Editorial Imprenta Casas, 1969); López y Rivas, *Los chicanos: una minoría nacional explotada* (Mexico D.F.: Nuestro Tiempo, 1971); López y Rivas, *La guerra de 47 y la resistencia popular a la ocupación* (Mexico D.F.: Editorial Nuestro Tiempo, 1976); Agustín Cué Cánovas, *Los Estados Unidos y el México Olvidado* (Mexico D.F.: Costa Amic, 1970).

[32] Juan Gómez-Quiñones, *La clase obrera en la historia de México: al norte del río bravo: pasado lejado—1600-1930.* (México D.F.: Siglo Veintiuno, 1981); David Maciel, *La clase obrera en la historia de México: al norte del río bravo: pasado inmediato—1930-1981.* (México D.F.: Siglo Veintiuno, 1981). Some of the earlier Chicano histories were David Maciel and Patricia Bueno, eds., *Aztlán: historia contemporañea del pueblo chicano* (Mexico D.F.: Secretaría de Educación Pública, 1976); also edited by Maciel and Bueno, *Azltán: historia del pueblo chicano, 1848-1910* (Mexico D.F.: SepSetentas, 1975); Juan Gómez-Quiñones, *Origenes de movimiento obrero chicano* (Mexico D.F.: Ediciones Era, 1978).

[33] David J. Weber, *La frontera norte de México, 1821-1846: el sudoeste norte americano en su época mexicana* (México D.F.: Fondo de Cultura Económica, 1988).

[34] Oscar Martínez, *Troublesome Border* (Tucson: University of Arizona Press, 1988), p.145.

[35] Richard Griswold del Castillo, *The Treaty of Guadalupe Hidalgo: A Legacy of Conflict* (Norman: University of Oklahoma Press, 1990).

[36] Juan Ramón García, *Operation Wetback: The Mass Deportation of Mexican Undocumented Workers in 1954* (Westport, Connecticut: Greenwood Press, 1980).

[37] Francisco Balderrama, *In Defense of La Raza: The Los Angeles Mexican Consulate and the Mexican Community, 1929-1936* (Tucson: University of Arizona Press, 1983); Robert R. Alvarez, Jr., *Familia: Migration and Adaptation in Baja and Alta California, 1800-1975* (Berkely, Los Angeles, and London: University of California Press, 1987); Abraham Hoffman, *An Oklahoma Tragedy* (El Paso: Texas Western Press/University of Texas, 1987).

THE IMPACT OF SENIORITY PRINCIPLES ON THE STATUS OF MEXICAN STEELWORKERS IN THE MIDWEST: HISTORICAL PERSPECTIVES

Jorge Hernandez-Fujigaki

Introduction

The March 1937 agreement between the U.S. Steel subsidiary, Carnegie-Illinois, and the Steel Workers Organizing Committee (SWOC), which was later to become the United Steel Workers of America (USWA), is considered a momentous event in the history of the labor movement in the United States. After U.S. Steel, the citadel of anti-unionism capitulated, the other steel corporations either accepted or anticipated the provisions of the Carnegie-Illinois contract.[1]

The agreement was of unprecedented importance. It recognized the SWOC as a collective bargaining agent, provided for the forty-hour week, eight-hour day, and time-and-a-half for all overtime. It specified a five dollar daily minimum wage and proportional increases in the brackets above the minimum. It also established a grievance system for workers' complaints, and introduced the principle of seniority for upgrades, promotions, demotions, layoffs, recalls, and vacations.[2]

The inclusion of the seniority principle in the contract, in the context of an industry convulsed by continuous seasonal, technological, and cyclical changes, was undoubtedly of major significance to the steelworkers. The seniority provisions promised a protective shield against hiring, upgrading, and training workers on the basis of kinship connections, while protecting older workers and union activists against arbitrary dismissals or reprisals.[3] Conceivably, seniority also protected against the use of racial/ethnic criteria in the hiring, promotion, training, or layoff of workers.[4] Thus, the incorporation of this principle into the new union contract was hailed as a major victory for American workers.

Unionists from different political persuasions reached common ground, agreeing on the benefits of the seniority provisions. Trade unionists and communists agreed that the last hired should be the first to go, and the last to go should be the first returned to work. The consolidation of the workforce in an industry with very high turnover rates would facilitate organizing campaigns.

Raymond Walsh, who wrote a sympathetic account of the early period of the Congress of International Organizations (CIO), supported seniority stipulations, arguing that:

> The employer wants freedom to hire the best available man when times are good, and to fire the least efficient man when times are bad, thus keeping his costs at a minimum. But it is a policy which places the burden of unemployment on the weak, the least capable, and refuses to protect the older man whose very loyalty of service has rendered him least prepared to change occupations.[5]

On the communist side, William Z. Foster, a leading figure in the steel strike of 1919, asserted that the seniority provisions protected older workers and prevented the arbitrary discharge of militant unionists. He also believed that economic depression and massive unemployment made seniority provisions even more imperative.[6]

However, while in theory the principle of seniority appeared to embody democracy, in the practical context it institutionalized the income and job security differentials between Whites and the predominantly unskilled and semi-skilled minorities. For one, the workers with the shortest period of employment and the least skills were Mexicans and Blacks, while the most experienced were native- and foreign-born Whites.[7] Thus, Whites obtained greater access to apprenticeships, skilled occupations, and increased protection against layoffs or "bumpings."

The late entry of Mexicans into the mills is only one element that explains their low occupational status. Once hired, Mexicans were channeled into departments with a high proportion of unskilled, low-paying jobs, and their advancement into skilled jobs and better-paying departments was limited by the very seniority provisions that were meant to protect all workers.

Establishment of Occupational Patterns
for Mexicans in the Steel Centers of the Midwest

By the time the SWOC launched its organizational campaigns, Mexicans were already one of the steel industry's primary sources of unskilled labor. The disruption of migration from Europe to the United States caused by the outbreak of World War I, plus increasing production for military purposes, and mounting labor unrest, which culminated in the Great Steel Strike of 1919, sent steel corporations out in a frantic search for alternative sources of unskilled labor. Southern Blacks and Mexicans became the most likely alternatives.

If the war created severe labor shortages and the steel strike created the juncture for the importation of Mexicans, the uprooting force which provided the industries of the urban Midwest with much-needed unskilled laborers was the Mexican Revolution. The impact of the revolution, especially after 1914, was felt in the Bajio area of West Central Mexico, from which the majority of the early immigrants to Chicago and Northwest Indiana came.[8]

Intensive recruitment of Mexican nationals between 1919 and 1925 by major steel manufacturers such as U.S. Steel, Youngstown Sheet & Tube, and Inland Steel transformed these immigrants overnight into an important part of the local work force. By 1928, Mexicans already constituted 12.5 percent of the 44,073 steel and metal workers employed by companies in this area. Inland Steel alone employed 2,000 of the 5,495 Mexicans.[9]

The occupational patterns established for Mexicans in the pre-CIO period (1919-1937) placed them as common laborers in the blast and open hearth furnaces, rolling mills and yard sections.[10] Some of the occupations assigned to them were those of chippers, heater's helpers, and third helpers.[11] Paul Taylor, in his seminal study of Mexican industrial workers in Chicago and Northwest Indiana, noticed in the early 1930s that the overwhelming majority of the Mexican steel and metal workers at seven area plants were unskilled.[12] Table 1, below, shows the distribution of skills among Mexicans, based on Taylor's criteria, at U.S. Steel's subsidiary Illinois Steel Company in South Chicago and Gary, Indiana. He considered these data as "fairly representative" of the occupational status of Mexicans in five other large steel plants in the area.[13]

TABLE 1:
Distribution of Skills Among Mexicans and Total Employees at U.S. Steel Gary Works and South Works, 1928

	Total Number of Employees	Percent	Total Number of Mexicans	Percent
Skilled	8,101	36.7	38	1.8
Semi-skilled	5,704	25.9	397	19.1
Unskilled	8,256	37.4	1,646	79.1
TOTAL	22,061	100.0	2,081	100.0

Source: Paul S. Taylor, *Mexican Labor in the United States: Chicago and the Calumet Region* (Berkeley: University of California Press, 1932), p. 157.

Taylor's data revealed that 79 percent of all Mexicans were un-skilled, compared to 37 percent of workers overall. While 37 percent of all workers were skilled, this was true for less than two percent of Mexicans.[14] The semi-skilled, who represented a little over 19 percent of the Mexicans, included occupations such as railway switchmen and roll hand. The skilled, representing less than two percent, included, among others, painters, molders and electric welders.[15]

By 1928, Mexicans, with a relatively short record of service in steel, were already voicing their complaints against the hiring and promo-tional practices of their immediate supervisors, most of whom were of Slavic background. They complained of being given the dirtiest and hardest work, and charged that foremen showed favoritism toward members of their own ethnic groups. Some Mexicans believed that they were assigned to the ". . .most dangerous work and the lowest paid jobs."[16] A steel company representative acknowledged the discriminatory practices of his foremen, stating that: ". . .we have Polish, Austrian, and Lithuanian foremen who prefer their own people."[17] Thus, it was not an uncommon practice of low-level and middle managers to make job assignments based on both the perceived skills and ethnic-racial background of workers. A Mexican who exonerated top management from any wrongdoing laid the blame of discrimination on his immediate supervisors: "The *mayor-domos* (foremen) make distinctions. They give the Mexicans the heavy work and the Poles *suave* (light) work with better pay. The office makes no distinction."[18]

In some instances, management's hiring practices were so fine tuned that Mexican job applicants were screened according to the color of their skin. A manager of a large steel plant stated:

> When I hire Mexicans at the gate I pick out the lightest among them. No, it isn't that the lighter-colored ones are any better workers, but the darker ones are like the niggers. When some of our contractors who came from the outside to do work for us used Negroes, I noticed the attitude of our men when they ate in the company cafeteria. So I chose Mexicans instead of Negroes, and in order to minimize feelings of race friction and keep away from the color line as far as possible, I employ only the lighter-colored Mexicans.[19]

In contrast to this pragmatic approach, other steel managers favored the hiring of light-skinned Mexicans because they considered them more racially akin to Whites: "The Castilian Mexicans are more intelligent than the darker Indians. . .You can tell those with Negro blood. They seem to be thicker through the temples and duller."[20]

Management's Evaluation Criteria and Departmental Seniority Systems

With the unionization of the major steel companies, the seniority provisions became a standard criteria when considering layoffs or promotions. If competence (i.e., knowledge, training, ability, skill, efficiency, physical fitness), family status and place of residency were relatively equal, then length of continuous service became the governing factor. Family status (marital status, number of dependents) and worker's place of residence, for example, became irrelevant unless length of service and competence were relatively equal. A typical clause stated:

> It is understood and agreed that in all cases of promotion or increase or decrease of forces, the following factors shall be considered, and where factors (b), (c), (d), and (e) are relatively equal, length of continuous service shall govern.
>
> (a) Length of continuous service
> (b) Knowledge, training, ability, skill and efficiency
> (c) Physical fitness
> (d) Family status; number of dependents, etc.
> (e) Place of residence[21]

Thus, in practice, seniority and the perceived competence of a worker were considered the main evaluation criteria for the managers of the steel companies. It was in the interpretation of competence that the subjective evaluations of supervisors became paramount for the assignment of a worker to his "rightful place" at the mill. While a worker's length of service might be objectively determined by a manager, it was more difficult to rate his competence without any preconceived bias or favoritism.

The subjective evaluations made by the immediate supervisors and by the general foreman of a department—most of whom were White—about whom to lay off, train or promote proved to be prejudicial to Mexicans, and later to Chicanos and other Latinos. Managers made their evaluations in the context of an occupational pyramid in which Mexicans had been positioned at the very bottom for a long time and were already identified with menial occupations. They were virtually kept out of skilled jobs because there was no set precedent of their efficiency as skilled workers and craftsmen.

Their cumulative experience in the mills, which had made them excellent chippers, scarfers, hookers, and other general laborers, was now hindering their chances of being considered suitable candidates for skilled occupations such as electrician, mechanic, roller, pipefitter and welder.[22] Thus, the occupations traditionally held by Mexicans served as informal identifiers, influencing management assignment and promotion decisions.[23]

The realization that long job tenure did not automatically insure upgrading or promotion if not accompanied by positive management evaluations led a Mexican worker at Inland to note in 1956:

> They can't fire a Mexican like they used to. The union protects them. . .we have seniority now, but I've seen departments where Mexican men have high seniority but the representation of the union doesn't do anything for them. They don't get the same chances for promotion.[24]

The status of Mexican, Chicano, and other Latino workers could be further viewed in the context of the distinction between plant-wide and departmental seniority. Beginning in 1937 and until the mid-1970s, seniority within a job classification or department was the determinant for promotion, transfer opportunities, protection against layoffs, recall rights, and access to training in the steel industry.[25]

Although seniority computed on a plant- or company-wide basis was taken into account during layoffs or recalls, the key factor in determining the status of a worker vis-à-vis his co-workers was ultimately his departmental and sequence seniority.[26]

After the managers of steel companies assigned a worker to a department, the worker could initiate admittance into a promotional sequence by his own request. Afterwards, his advancement within a given occupation was controlled by his position in the seniority totem called "sequence seniority." He usually entered the sequence at the lowest paid levels of an occupation, and began competing for better paid or more desirable jobs based on his entry date. Thus, a department had different seniority sequences, depending on the variety, complexity and size of its operations. For instance, Inland's Steel Blast Furnace Department, in 1956, had the following sequences: "dock mechanical," "ore bridge operators," "dock cleaner," "pig machine," "foundry," "general labor," "millwright," "pipefitter," "electrical," "furnace well," "stockhouse," "highline," and "miscellaneous maintenance."[27]

Promotion policies compelled a worker to enter a sequence in the bottom job. From there he had to push his way up through various layers of jobs before he was finally allowed access to a job he wanted or for which he was qualified, irrespective of his plant-wide seniority. Thus, a worker who was allowed to use his seniority to bid on jobs in his own department was denied the opportunity to use it plant-wide.

The seniority provisions of the contract penalized workers who transferred, with a loss of the seniority in their old departments, after thirty days. In addition, transferred workers were subjected to what amounted to a demotion. They were compelled to start at the bottom of the occupational sequence in their new departments, becoming juniors of fellow workers with less plant-wide seniority.[28] For Mexicans, Chicanos, and Puerto Ricans, the above seniority stipulations became a powerful deterrent that confined them to opportunities offered by the department to which managers had originally assigned them. These groups were able to advance up the seniority totem, but not in proportion to their presence in the workforce.

Mexicans in the Steel Mills: The Case of Inland Steel

The combined impact of informal management tracking systems and USWA-sponsored seniority provisions on Mexicans and other Latinos can be viewed by focusing on Inland—historically, one of the largest industrial employers of this group in the Midwest. By the early 1960s this company was the third largest steel maker in the United States (6,700,000 net ingot tons annually). The 22,000 members of USWA's Local 1010 made it the largest steel local in the country.[29]

Inland, as a case study, offers the opportunity to extrapolate data. The fact that the USWA established an industry-wide pattern of collective bargaining meant that all the big steel corporations had virtually identical contractual provisions. Such similarities make the experiences of Mexicans and other Latinos at Inland useful in gaining an understanding of the experiences of members of this group at other firms.[30]

In a survey of personnel records from the years 1955-56, now at the Calumet Regional Archives at Indiana University Northwest, the following data on Spanish-surnamed workers were obtained (data were available on 2,640 workers, or 68 percent of the total with Spanish surnames). Table 2 shows the distribution of "helper" positions held by Spanish-surnamed workers at Inland's Open Hearth #1 and Open Hearth #3 in 1956. "Helpers" were a category of workers who assisted melters, a group of skilled workers responsible for the quality of steel produced in the open hearth furnaces.[31] Latinos represented 20 percent of Inland's overall workforce of 18,820 (3,877 workers) and 37.5 percent of the total number of workers in Open Hearth #1 and Open Hearth #3 (157 workers). Yet, only 2.1 percent of "first helpers" were Latinos. In startling contrast, more than two thirds of the "third helper" category, which required the least skill, was occupied by Latinos, as were more than one third of the semi-skilled "second helper" positions.[32]

TABLE 2:
Distribution of Latino Helpers in Inland Steel
Open Hearths #1 and #3, 1956

Occupations in Sequence	Total Number of Workers	Total Number of Latinos	Percent Latinos
First Helper	142	3	2.1
Second Helper	138	60	43.4
Third Helper	138	94	68.1
TOTAL	418	157	37.5

Source: USWA Local 1010 Records, Box #6, Continuous Service Lists, 1955-1956 (Gary, Calumet Regional Archives).

Lengthy stays at Inland helps explain the status of the three Latino first helpers, a more skilled position at Open Hearth #3. Mexicans had been concentrated in the labor pool of the open hearth sections since the early 1920s, and thus were at the top of the seniority lists.

Table 3 shows that even in those departments where Latinos were concentrated, some occupations were out of reach, such as those of the essentially lily-White Mechanical Division. The Inspection, Electrical and Crane Division did not fare better. Out of a combined labor force of 113 workers, only three were Latinos, including two out of 75 in the Inspection Division, none out of 10 in the Electrical, and none out of 28 in the Crane Division.[33]

TABLE 3:

Number of Latino and Non-Latino Workers in Inland Steel Open Hearth #3 Mechanical Division, 1956

Occupation	Number of Non-Latinos	Number of Latinos
Crane Repairman (1st Class)	3	0
Mobile Equipment Repairman (1st Class)	3	0
Mobile Equipment Repairman (2nd Class)	2	0
Welder Combination (1st Class)	3	0
Boiler Maker (1st Class)	1	0
Millwright (1st Class)	5	1
Maintenance Day Pipefitter	1	0
Turn Pipefitter	4	0
TOTAL	22	1

Source: USWA Local 1010 Records, Box # 6, Continuous Service Lists, 1955-1956 (Gary, Calumet Regional Archives).

Table 4, below, which includes the craft and maintenance occupations of six work areas and one department (Open Hearths #1, #2 and #3, Cold Strip #2, Galvanizing, Mechanical, Blast Furnaces) shows that, overall, Latinos had made very modest inroads in traditionally White-dominated occupations. By 1956, 14 years after the USWA obtained its first contract from Inland, Latinos, who as a group had a service record of 36 years, had barely penetrated the traditional turf of the White craftsmen.

TABLE 4:
Number of Latinos and Non-Latinos in Craft
and Maintenance Occupations, 1956

Occupation	Number of Non-Latinos	Number of Latinos	Percent Latinos
Motor Inspector (Maintenance)	150	4	2.6
Pipefitter (Craft & Maintenance)	49	2	4.8
Millwright (Maintenance)	86	7	8.1
Welder (Craft & Maintenance)	49	6	12.2
Roll Turner (Craft)	48	0	0
Boilermaker (Craft & Maintenance)	12	0	0
Rigger (Craft & Maintenance)	8	3	37.5
Blacksmith (Craft & Maintenance)	4	1	25.0
TOTAL	406	23	5.6

Source: USWA Local 1010 Records, Box # 6, Continuous Service Lists, 1955-1956 (Gary, Calumet Regional Archives).

In Table 5, the breakdown of crafts and maintenance occupations into three major categories ("first class," "second class" and "helpers") allows for a closer look at the standing of Latinos within the crafts and other skilled jobs.[34] Out of a total of 21 Latinos found in these jobs, only slightly over one-half (11) had first-class status, five were second-class and five were helpers).

TABLE 5:
Categories of Latinos Within Craft
and Maintenance Occupations, 1956

Occupation	Total Number of Latinos	First Class	Second Class	Helpers
Motor Inspector	4	2	2	0
Pipefitter	2	1	1	0
Millwright	7	2	0	5
Welders	6	4	2	0
Rigger	Information Not Available			
Blacksmith	1	1	0	0
TOTAL	21	11	5	5

Source: USWA Local l0l0 Records, Box # 6, Continuous Service Units, l955-1956 (Gary, Calumet Regional Archives).

Table 6 shows the effects of management's initial job assignment system on Latino workers at Inland Steel. By l956, the majority of the 2,640 Latinos covered by this survey were concentrated in seven of 22 areas in the company.[35] By the mid-l950s, the assignment of newly-hired Latinos to unskilled occupations in the open hearths, rolling mills, transportation areas and yards—which Paul Taylor had noticed as far back as the early l930s—was a well-established pattern. In sharp contrast, in departments and shops where operations required large numbers of craftsmen and other skilled workers (Mechanical, Stores and Refractories, Power & Steam & Combustion, Quality Control, Carpenter and Blacksmith shops), Latinos were under-represented, or not represented at all.

TABLE 6:
Distribution of Latinos at Inland Steel, 1956
(9 Work Areas, 2 Departments and 3 Shops)

Area/Department	Total Number of Workers	Number of Latinos	Percent Latinos
Open Hearth #1	702	305	43.4
Open Hearth #2	1748	728	41.6
Open Hearth #3	694	351	50.5
Transportation & Yards	933	521	55.8
44 & 76 Hot Strip Mill & #3 Blooming Mill	1563	408	26.1
Field Forces	848	161	18.9
Mechanical Department	749	52	6.9
Stores & Refractories	366	37	10.1
Power & Steam & Combustion	464	33	7.1
Quality Control	414	19	4.5
Machine Shop	295	17	5.7
Blacksmith Shop	63	8	12.6
Carpenter Shop	37	0	0
Electrical Department	68	0	0
TOTAL	8869	2640	29.7

Source: USWA Local 1010 Records, Box # 6, Continuous Service Lists, 1955-1956 (Gary, Calumet Regional Archives).

In the context of an industry that had traditionally assigned Latinos and other minorities to unskilled occupations, the departmental seniority provisions became the USWA's main Achilles' heel in its quest for the reduction of inequalities between its predominantly White craftsmen and its largely unskilled and semi-skilled minority members.

Herbert Hill, an expert on the impact of racial conflict in the workplace and in labor relations, goes as far as to state that CIO-endorsed departmental seniority provisions, testing devices, and unrelated job qualifications kept Blacks and other minorities out of the best paid and more skilled occupations, perhaps as effectively as the old craft unions had through White-only membership provisions, racially biased licensing boards and apprenticeship programs that favored White applicants. Hill concludes that "as black workers in the steel industry, in pulp and paper manufacturing, in oil and chemical refineries, in tobacco factories and in other industries have learned, what exclusion is to craft unions, separate lines of promotion and seniority are to the industrial unions."[36]

The Steel Manual *for Job Classifications and Latinos*

Beginning in 1937, the contract seniority provisions formally established the elusive criteria of competence ("knowledge, training, ability, skill and efficiency") for promotions and layoffs. In matters of wages, a counterpart was found in the *Manual for Job Classifications,* commonly known as the *Steel Manual,* which went into effect in February of 1947. The implementation of the *Manual's* new guidelines to rate the perceived worth of jobs in the steel industry helped eliminate the pronounced wage disparities among workers performing similar functions, and in some instances helped reduce wage differences among various categories of workers. The *Steel Manual* classified and approved benchmark jobs into a wage scale with 30 standard wage classifications. It used 12 factors to rate the perceived worth of jobs according to their content, as seen in Table 7. The *Manual* became paramount in determining the perceived competency, and thus, the earning levels, of various categories of workers.

TABLE 7:
Steel Manual Rating Factors for Job Classifications, 1947

Factor	Maximum Weight of factor
(1) Pre-employment training	1.0
(2) Employment training and experience	4.0
(3) Mental skill	3.5
(4) Manual skill	2.0
(5) Responsibility for materials	10.0
(6) Responsibility for tools and equipment	4.0
(7) Responsibility for operation	6.5
(8) Responsibility for safety of others	2.0
(9) Mental effort	2.5
(10) Physical effort	2.5
(11) Surroundings	3.0
(12) Hazards	2.0

Source: Robert Tilove, "The Wage Rationalization Program in the United States," *Monthly Labor Review,* June 1947, pp. 967-979

The steel companies and the USWA gave the highest rating, over 50 percent of the total points, to "responsibility" factors. As a result, the top members of the crew—all craft or skilled workers—were given special treatment. While craft jobs, such as machinist and roller, received considerable credit, occupations in which Latinos were over-represented, such as laborer, stocker and chipper, were given the lowest ratings.

Little weight was given to the "physical effort" and "hazards," that common laborers performed and endured under dangerous condi-tions. If properly recognized, these factors could have received higher marks. However, their actual assigned weights illustrate a set of values inclined to favor craft jobs. An ultimate effect of these rating factors was to sanction the primacy of the knowledge and skills of the predominantly White craftsmen and skilled workers, to the detriment of the largely unskilled Mexican, Latino, and Black workers.[37]

Conclusions

The manner in which the seniority provisions became operative after management had exercised its job assignment prerogatives did not offer unskilled Latinos any substantive hope of moving out of their menial occupations. On the contrary, it encouraged them to remain in the departments of their initial assignment. Under these cir-cumstances, rather than transfer to other lines of work, Latinos largely opted to stay in those occupations and departments where they were heavily concentrated and to try to advance within the occupational ladders available in those sections. Therefore, it was more common to seek intra-departmental rather than inter-departmental transfers.

As a consequence of the above, most Latinos were not exposed to a wide range of occupations in such areas as the mechanical, electrical and maintenance departments, or the carpenter and machine shops. This severely limited their capacity to gain qualifications outside of their traditional sections.

Racially and ethnically biased hiring and assignment practices, largely unchallenged by the leadership of the USWA, together with subjective job evaluations helped perpetuate inequalities between Whites and Latinos in the steel mills. The seniority provisions of the collective agreements in the SWOC-USWA era ultimately cemented an occupational hierarchy that kept Latinos at the bottom.

NOTES

[1] Robert R.R. Brooks, *As Steel Goes: Unionism in a Basic Industry* (New Haven: Yale University Press, l940), pp. 110-129, 242-260; I. W. Abel, *Collective Bargaining, Labor Relations in Steel: Then and Now* (New York: Columbia University Press for Carnegie-Mellon University, 1976); United Steel Workers of America, Education Department. *Then and Now: The Story of the United Steelworkers of America* (n.p., l974).

[2] William T. Hogan, *Economic History of the Iron and Steel Industry in the United States.* 5 Vols. (Lexington, Massachusetts.: Lexington Books, 1971), Vol. III, pp. 1173-1178.; Edward Robert Livernash, *Collective Bargaining in the Basic Steel Industry* (Washington: United States Department of Labor, 1961), pp. 231-234; Frederick H. Harbinson, *Collective Bargaining in the Steel Industry: 1937* (Princeton: Princeton University, 1938), pp. 1-9.

[3] Brooks, *As Steel Goes,* pp. 217-240.

[4] Raymond J. Walsh, *CIO, Industrial Unionism in Action* (New York: W.W. Norton & Co., 1937), pp. 125, 233; Brooks, *Ibid.*

[5] Walsh, *Ibid.,* p. 126

[6] Although Foster did welcome the inclusion of seniority provisions into the union contracts, he advised workers ". . .to check possible abuses and to protect the place of the youth in industry. Seniority rules must not be used to discriminate against the employment of Negroes." William Z. Foster, *American Trade Unionism: Principles, Organization, Strategy, Tactics* (New York: International Publishers, 1970), pp. 283-284.

[7] In this paper, the term "Mexican" refers to those individuals born and/or raised in Mexico. "Chicano" refers to individuals of Mexican ancestry born and/or raised in the United States. Finally, "Latinos" refers to individuals who can trace their ancestry to Latin America, regardless if they were born or raised in the United States or in Latin America. In 1948, U.S. Steel's recruitment of 500 Puerto Rican islanders to work as laborers at the Gary Works marked the true diversification of the Latino community in Chicago and Northwest Indiana. (*Gary Post Tribune,* June 7, 1948, p. 1).

[8] Francisco A. Rosales, "Mexican Immigration to the Urban Midwest During the 1920's" (Ph.D. dissertation, Indiana University, 1978), pp. 98-99.

[9] Paul S. Taylor, *Mexican Labor in the United States: Chicago and the Calumet Region* (Berkeley: University of California Press, 1932), pp. 34-37, 67; Rosales, *Ibid.,* p. 176.

[10] The blast furnaces are the first major productive units in the steel industry, as they transform iron into molten metal. The blast furnace is "essentially a tapered, giant cylindrical steel shell lined with refractory brick, [that]. . .reduces the iron content of the ore to a relatively pure metal called pig iron. This is accomplished by introducing three basic materials, iron ore, coke and limestone at the top of a vertical shaft or stack. . . ." Hogan, *op. cit.,* Vol. II, p. 391.

The open furnaces perform the second major operation in steelmaking. Indeed, the actual process of steel manufacturing begins when the materials (molten pig iron, scrap and other raw materials) are loaded into open hearth furnaces to produce steel ingots (*Ibid.*, p. 408).

The rolling mills are usually the last major productive phase in the steelmaking process. The steel ingots are reheated for shaping into finished products such as steel wire, structural steel girders and metal plate. William Kornblum, *Blue Collar Community* (Chicago: University of Chicago Press, 1974), p. 37.

Finally, the yards are a network of narrow and standard gauge tracks connecting the departments with each other and with the railroad tracks of the main line. It is in the yards where materials are piled and loaded onto trains. To operate this transportation machinery and keep the yards and tracks clean, a large number of workers is required.

[11] Chippers in foundries used a hammer and cold chisel, or a pneumatic chisel to remove surface impurities from steel products. A heater's helper was a laborer in the blast furnaces. Third helpers were laborers assigned to the open hearth furnaces who performed various strenuous tasks such as shoveling limestone and other materials into the sweltering furnaces, weighing charges, and cleaning up work areas. As late as 1942, the task of mixing was done by hand because there were no mechanical devices. United States Department of Labor, *Dictionary of Occupational Titles,* Volume 1 (Washington, D.C.: U.S. Government Printing Office, 1939), pp. 173, 445, 450; *Steel Shavings 7,* (Gary, IN: Indiana University Northwest), p. 18.

[12] The seven plants analyzed by Taylor were Gary Works and South Works (U.S. Steel), Tin Mill-American Sheet & Tin Plate Company, Inland Steel, Wisconsin Steel, National Tube and McCormick Works (Taylor, *Mexican Labor in the United States* pp. 36-37).

[13] *Ibid.,* p. 156.

[14] The main duties of the unskilled consisted ". . .largely either in handling the materials and products of the different processes or in cleaning up the waste, such as slag and scrap, which accumulates in tremendous quantities in all the departments." (U.S. Bureau of Labor Statistics, *Report on Conditions of Employment in the Iron and Steel Industry in the United States.* 4 Vols. (Washington: Government Printing Office, 1913), Vol. III, p. 82.

[15] The duties of a railway switchman (brakeman) were the switching and stopping of railroad cars in order to load or unload them. A roll hand or rolling-forging operator used a roller-die machine to forge heated iron bars into specified shapes. Finally, a molder was described as a worker who "makes molds for bulky castings on foundry floor by packing and ramming green sand, dry sand, or loam around patterns which have been placed in suitable flasks." *Dictionary of Occupational Titles,* pp. 99, 607, 755.

[16] Taylor, *Op. cit.,* p. 102.

[17] *Ibid.,* p. 92.

[18] *Ibid.,* p. 101.

[19] *Ibid.*, p. 110.

[20] *Ibid.*

[21] Harbison, *Op. cit.*, p. 19; Hogan, *Op. cit.*, p. 1175; Livernash, *Op. cit.*, p. 233; United Steelworkers of America, *Steel Labor* (March 20, 1937), p. 2; Agreement Between the United Steel Corporation and the United Steel Workers of America: Production and Maintenance Employees, Central Operations, Steel, (Pittsburgh, PA, 1956), p. 62; Agreement Between Inland Steel Company and the United Steel Workers of America, Local Union No. 1010 (Indiana Harbor, IN, 1945), pp. 33-36.

[22] The main responsibility of a scarfer was to tend rolls through which skelp (steel strips for making pipe or tube) or steel sheet was run prior to its being formed into tube. A hooker, also called crane follower or chainer, was a laborer who assisted a crane operator by affixing rope, cable, or chain sling to the object being lifted. *Dictionary of Occupational Titles,* pp. 244, 794.

[23] Taylor quoted the employment manager of a steel plant as saying that "The Mexicans are the best class of labor we get now. They are better than the colored or the south Europeans, though not than the old north Europeans. They are a nice class of people to handle. If the American people will just treat them right, we'll have a fine class of people and a fine class of labor. They stand heat well and stand hard work. We find a number of big strong Mexicans who are as able as the others to do the work requiring strength." Taylor, *Op. cit.*, p. 89.

[24] Joel Seidman, *The Worker Views His Union* (Chicago: University of Chicago Press, 1956), p. 81.

[25] In April 1974, the federal government filed a consent decree with nine steel companies and the USWA. The government determined that Blacks, women and Latinos "were systematically assigned to lower-paying jobs with little opportunity for advancement, denied training opportunities, and judged by more stringent qualification criteria than were White males." The decree committed U.S. Steel, Republic, Youngstown Sheet and Tube, Bethlehem, Jones and Laughin, National Steel, Wheeling-Pittsburgh Steel, Armco Steel and Allegheny-Ludlum to pay $30.5 million to 34,449 Black and Latino steelworkers and to 5,559 women employees hired before 1968. Ray Marshall, *Employment Discrimination: The Impact of Legal and Administrative Remedies* (New York, Praeger Publishers, 1978) p. 7; United Steel Workers of America, *Evaluating The Steel Industry* (Pittsburgh, 1976), p. 12.

In addition, the USWA was forced to acknowledge its role in employment discrimination against Blacks, Latinos and women. The consent decree also specified goals and set up timetables for the hiring and promotion of members of the above groups to supervisory, technical, and clerical jobs, and in company-sponsored training programs. Another important provision was the replacement of departmental seniority with plant-wide seniority as the criteria for promotions, demotions, layoffs and recalls in the industry (*Ibid.*).

[26] William B. Gould, *Black Workers in White Unions: Job Discrimination in the United States* (Ithaca: Cornell University Press, 1977), p. 67; Equal Employment Opportunity Commission, "Powell et. al. *v.* Inland Steel Company and the United Steel Workers of America, et. al. TCH 4c-2599" (Washington, n.d.), p. 20; Frederick H.

Harbison, *The Seniority Principle in Union-Management Relations* (Princeton: Princeton University Press, 1939), pp. 12-13, 23, 25-26.

[27] Agreement Between Inland Steel Company and the United Steelworkers of America, Locals 1010 and 64, May 7, 1947, pp. 19-23; USWA Local 1010 Records, Collection 115, Box #6 (Gary, IN: Calumet Regional Archives).

[28] Agreement Between Inland Steel Company and USWA, Local Union 1010, May 7, 1947, p. 24.

[29] Julian Samora, *Mexican-Americans in a Midwest Metropolis: A Study of East Chicago* (Los Angeles, University of California, Los Angeles. Mexican American Study Project. Advanced Report 8. 1967), p. 11.

[30] Since the SWOC period (1936-42), the United Steel Corporation established the pattern of settlements which the other steel firms would follow. However, the highly centralized nature of the bargaining process and the consequent propensity toward standardization of settlements throughout the industry should not lead to the conclusion that the contracts of the different steel firms were mere carbon copies of the U.S. Steel contract. On the contrary: "There have been frequent variations from the U.S. Steel settlement on both wage and non-wage items to meet special situations, and there were occasions when a company other than U.S. Steel led in the settlement." Livernach, *Op. cit.*, p. 86.

[31] The highly skilled melters worked in a section where scrap iron was melted and purified. They decided when each furnace was ready to pour by observing the color of the molten metal through cobalt-blue glasses and by referring to carbon tests of the metal made by the First Helpers. The assistants of the latter group of workers, the Second Helpers, worked under extremely hot conditions when near the furnace, weighing the scrap iron and loading it into charging boxes. They locked the charging boxes, inserted them into the furnace, and manipulated the control which dumped the charge. *Dictionary of Occupational Titles,* pp. 527, 839, 1171, 1372.

[32] Inland Steel Company. *Employment Characteristics, Human Resources Information Management.* (East Chicago, IN: Inland Steel Department of Personnel, 1990).

[33] USWA Local 1010 Records, Box No. 6, Continuous Service Lists, 1955-1956 (Gary, IN. Calumet Regional Archives).

[34] In this case "helper" refers to a strata of workers, usually with very few skills, who assisted the semi-skilled or skilled workers by supplying them with materials and tools, cleaning working areas, machines and equipment. United States Department of Labor, *Dictionary of Occupational Titles,* Volume 1 (Washington, D.C.: Government Printing Office, 1949), p. 659.

[35] Inland Steel's 22 work areas included: Blast Furnace, Coke Plant, Plant No. 3, No. 1 Open Hearth, No. 2 Open Hearth, Power & Steam & Combustion, No. 2 Bloomer, 10" & 14" Mills, Plant No. 1 Mills, Plate Mill & Silo Road, Galvanize, 76" Hot Strip, 44" & 76" Slab Yard & No. 3 Bloomer, 44" Hot Strip, Cold Strip, Tin Mill, Transportation & Yards, Field Forces, Stores & Refractories, Quality Control, No. 3 Open Hearth. *Local 1010 Steelworker,* Vol. 2, No. 6 (Gary, IN. Calumet Regional Archives).

[36] Herbert Hill, *Black Labor and the American Legal System: Race, Work and the Law* (Madison: The University of Wisconsin Press, 1985), p. 25.

[37] Hogan, *Op. cit.*, pp. 1189-1191; United Steel Workers of America and the United Steel Corporation *Job Description and Classification Manual* (n.p., 1953), pp. 5-10.; Inland Steel Company, *Job Description and Classification Manual: Basic Steel Operations* (n.p., 1963), pp. 6-13.

RURAL CHICANA/O COMMUNITIES AND THE ENVIRONMENT: AN ATTITUDINAL SURVEY OF RESIDENTS OF COSTILLA COUNTY, COLORADO

Devon Peña, Rubén Martinez, and Louis McFarland

Introduction

E nvironmental racism has recently received increased attention from activists, scholars, and policy makers.[1] Increasing numbers of studies are providing evidence of differential patterns of hazardous toxic waste dumping in minority and dominant-group communities and regions.[2] The Center for Third World Organizing cites a 1983 General Accounting Office study which indicates that in three out of every four cases, waste disposal and toxic waste sites are located in low-income, ethnic minority communities.[3] The Commission for Racial Justice found that three out of every five Black and Hispanic Americans reside in areas with uncontrolled toxic waste sites.[4] This racial (and class) feature of environmental degradation has often been overlooked by environmental activists, who tend to perceive ethnic minorities as more willing than Whites to trade environmental protection for the sake of jobs. For instance, a recent research proposal, entitled "Determining Why Minority Communities Demonstrate Little or No Interest in Environmental Issues," states:

> In over ten years of providing environmental education programs to schools, public audiences, professional and fraternal organizations, virtually no interest has been observed among minority

The authors thank Corpus Gallegos, Joe Gallegos, Praxedis Ortega, Jr., Felix Romero, Charles Manzanares, Charlie Jaquez, Maria Valdez, Sister Teresa Jaramillo, and Sister Marie Claire Manhart for their assistance and advice. Support for this study was provided to the first author by the Helen Hunt Jackson Faculty Fellows Program, Hulbert Center for Southwestern Studies, and a Benezet Research Grant from the Faculty Research and Development Board, Colorado College. The views expressed in this article are the sole responsibility of the authors.

audiences. Further research has determined that minority participation in both local and national natural history museums, zoos,
and environmental organizations is extremely limited.[5]

There is, in fact, a considerable social science literature that seeks
to determine why ethnic minorities do not participate in the environmental movement and why they appear less interested in environmental issues in general.[6] Critics of this research argue that the
problem is not with ethnic minority populations but with environmental organizations, which tend to reflect the concerns of their
predominantly White, middle-class constituencies.[7]

Laura Pulido has recently pointed out that:

> . . .[W]ithin both the literature and practice of institutional
> environmentalism, limited attention has been given to issues of
> poverty, inequity, and racism. This perception is compounded by
> the fact that the participants of institutional environmentalism are
> primarily middle-class and Anglo. . . .[The] environmental move-
> ment has drawn too sharp a line between humans and nature,
> thus blinding activists to the inherent connections between social
> justice and environmental protection.[8]

Perhaps minority and dominant groups perceive and focus on
environmental issues differently. It may be that mainstream environmentalists are concerned with the protection of wildlife and wilder-
ness areas, while ethnic minorities are more likely concerned with
environmental hazards found in their everyday living and working
spaces.[9] The problem seems to be one of sharp differences in the
definition and prioritization of policy agendas.

Another important dimension to the study of environmental racism
is the conflict between indigenous and dominant groups over control
and ownership of native lands and waters.[10] As capitalist dynamics
intensify in the hinterlands they pose increased threats to the lands
and waters once held, managed, and used by indigenous peoples in
accordance with their own traditions and practices.

In this study, the environmental attitudes of Chicanas/os in Costilla
County, Colorado, are examined.[11] Chicanas/os in northern New
Mexico and southern Colorado (also called the Upper Rio Grande
bioregion) are among the few population segments in this country
that continue to struggle to retain control over their native lands and
the natural resources found therein. Although separated by American-

imposed, geo-political boundaries, Chicanas/os on both sides of the New Mexico-Colorado state boundary are bound together by powerful historical, cultural, and kinship ties. For nearly two centuries, and until the conclusion of the American-Mexican War in 1848, the area of present-day Colorado that lies south of the Arkansas River was part of New Spain and, later, Mexico.[12] This area and its peoples formally became part of the U.S. New Mexico Territory in 1850. In 1861, this region became the southernmost part of the Colorado Territory. Because the earliest settlements in Colorado were established by New Mexicans moving northward from Taos and other northern New Mexico towns, the indelible cultural imprint made on the social and natural landscape was that by "New Mexican" Chicanas/os. These early settlements were established as relatively self-sufficient agricultural and ranching settlements.[13] Massive changes in land tenure and usage have taken place during this century which have left Chicana/o communities almost completely dependent upon social services provided by the dominant society.[14] Incorporation within the system of American capitalism resulted in the displacement of a mixed, cash and barter economy by a money economy. It also resulted in the transfer of millions of acres from Chicanas/os to "Americans" and their government, over-grazing and deforestation, soil erosion, and severely damaged watersheds.[15] Today, another capitalist onslaught is underway in the bioregion, with Chicanas/os overwhelmed by the intrusion of development, mining, and recreational companies that seem to commodify everything in their paths. This increased commodification of natural and cultural resources in the Upper Rio Grande bioregion threatens the cultural integrity and everyday lives of local Chicanas/os.[16] It is in this context that we explore the environmental attitudes of Chicanas/os in the bioregion.

Literature Review

Chicanas/os in northern New Mexico and southern Colorado are among the poorest population segments in this country.[17] Studies on this population have shown that members tend to hold a distinctive view of land that differs considerably from those of Anglos and other Americans. T. Atencio, a pioneer in the study of Chicanas/os and land utilization, argues that among this population segment land is directly related to being and life.[18] Rather than being a commodity, as typically seen by Americans, land among Chicanas/os in the Upper Rio Grande bioregion is home, and for some it is body and soul. This view forms the basis of a land ethic that some have characterized as a "lococentric" or place-centered cultural ecology.[19] A similar point is made by C. Knowlton, who wrote, "A very strong emotional attachment exists between the Spanish-American farmer or rancher and his land. He knows every physical characteristic of his land and regards it as a basic part of his small social and psychological world."[20] Within this cultural framework there is an emphasis on the maintenance and preservation of the environment based on the pragmatic view that the land will not yield much if it is not maintained well.

One of the first empirical studies focusing directly on Chicana/o attitudes toward land and land use is that by Eastman, Carruthers, and Liefer, who found that members of this population segment do indeed have an emotional attachment to the land.[21] Within their view, the land is part of the family. According to the authors of the study, this segment of the Chicana/o population "emphasize[s] land transfer-and-use decisions based upon community welfare. . ."[22] Eastman and his associates also found that education and commercial-mindedness were positively related among Chicanas/os, and that past or present land ownership and rural residence were positively related to the traditional view of land.

A more recent study by Brown and Ingram focusing on water rights and uses found that Chicana/o community leaders in the Upper Rio Grande bioregion tended to oppose the sale and lease of water rights.[23] This opposition, they argue, is grounded in social and cultural concerns rather than in economics. Upper Rio Grande Chicanas/os also tend to oppose recreational development, preferring instead agriculture and the production of wood products.[24]

Some scholars view the traditional attitudes and economic practices of these Chicanas/os as important for the development of the bioregion in ecologically sustainable ways. Van Dresser views their practices as ". . .uniquely suited for an evolutionary development towards the essential bioeconomic community in the future."[25] Van Ness argues that "If the land base of the villagers can be reestablished under the traditional tenure system, then regional economic networks could be rejuvenated without great effort or cost compared to the demands of conventional development programs."[26]

Empirical Generalizations

Using the findings from the foregoing studies we developed three generalizations to describe the environmental orientation of Chicanas/os in the Upper Rio Grande bioregion generally, and Costilla County in particular:

1) Chicanas/os in Costilla County exhibit critical attitudes toward land and water uses that they perceive as negatively impacting the community. Where the natural environment in the locality is harmed, the community is harmed.

2) Chicanas/os in Costilla County oppose the sale of water rights for commercial ventures, perceiving it as detrimental to the capacity of the land to produce.

3) Chicanas/os in Costilla County support economic development ventures that seem to them to benefit the community by being ecologically sustainable and respectful of the local cultural landscape.

We expect that the longer persons have resided in the region, the more they will abide by the local culture, and the more they will tend to hold these ecological attitudes.

The Context: Costilla County

Costilla County is located in the San Luis Valley in southern Colorado. It is one of seven contiguous, rural counties in northern New Mexico and southern Colorado which have Chicana/o majority populations.[27] There are approximately 3,190 persons living in Costilla County, with 2,452 (or 76.9 percent) being of Hispanic origin.[28] Like the other counties in this Indo-Hispano cultural region, Costilla County has a high unemployment rate (more than twice the state-wide average), a high rate of families living below the poverty threshold (35 percent, or four times the state-wide average), and a high rate of out-migration of families and unemployed or underemployed youth.[29] The county is decidedly bilingual; some estimates place Spanish-speaking ability at 95 percent of the Chicana/o population.[30]

The main sources of employment in Costilla County are the county and municipal governments, and the school district. Farming and ranching are the third most important sources of employment.[31] There are few jobs in manufacturing and construction. Mining, too, has played a negligible role in generating employment opportunities. Federal entitlement programs such as Aid to Families with Dependent Children (AFDC) and Social Security Supplemental Income (SSI) are important sources of income for at least one-third of the county's residents.

In recent times, the population has contended with mining operations in the area that have negatively impacted the environment or threaten to do so. For instance, Earth Sciences, Inc. (ESI), a mining company based in Golden, Colorado, operated a cyanide heap leach operation in the Rito Seco watershed. This watershed is located in the foothills of the Sangre de Cristo Mountains about three miles northeast of San Luis, the capitol of Costilla County. This watershed supports the oldest system of water usage rights in Colorado, *acequias* (irrigation ditches) with decrees dating back to the 1850s. On April 6, 1975, a cyanide spill into the Rito Seco produced a fish kill up to six miles downstream from the leach pad.[32] The Colorado Department of Health issued a cease and desist order. This was followed by a similar action by the Environmental Protection Agency (EPA) in October 1975. In October 1979, the Colorado Department of Health issued another cease and desist order and a "Cleanup Order and Notice of Violation of Previous Order." Also in October 1979, the EPA prevailed in a lawsuit against ESI and ordered the company to reclaim the cyanide leach pad area. The leach pad remains unreclaimed, and a clean-up has yet to be undertaken.[33]

In 1987, Battle Mountain Gold (BMG), a transnational mining corporation based in Houston, Texas, announced plans to develop a strip-mine and cyanide leaching operation in the same area mined by ESI. In December 1989, after lengthy regulatory hearings and court battles, BMG initiated strip-mining activities. BMG now mines for the microscopic specks of gold contained in a series of depositions in a pre-Cambrian basement rock stratum that lies below the Santa Fe Conglomerate. The conglomerate is associated with glacial retreat deposits and is a geological mass of heterogenous materials along the foothills of the Sangre de Cristo Mountains from southern Colorado all the way south to Santa Fe. This conglomerate is considered an "overburden waste" and must first be removed to a depth of up to several hundred feet before reaching the ore-bearing rock. The operation involves strip-mining and crushing the ore-bearing rock to the consistency of flour; the ore is then processed via an enclosed cyanide leach vat system designed to extract .032 ounces of gold per ton of crushed material. Considerable wastes and tailings are generated through this process, requiring the use of a 240-acre containment pond. This tailings pond is a major threat to the local watershed, and thus to the acequias and the farms and ranches that rely on the Rito Seco for some of their irrigation water.[34]

The strip-mining and cyanide-leaching proposal generated sharp opposition from local Chicano/a farmers, ranchers, and other water users who organized themselves as the Costilla County Committee for Environmental Soundness (CES) in November of 1988. The CES was established to:

> (1) protect the pristine and diverse ecology of Costilla County, (2) promote a healthy balance between agriculture, business, and the environment, and (3) encourage citizen involvement in efforts to keep the environment safe, beautiful, and conducive to the health of residents as well as plants and animals. . .The CES is thus committed to protecting natural and cultural diversity by linking ecological concerns with issues of social justice and equity.[35]

The CES is composed of local farmers, ranchers, clergy, educators, business persons, and community planners. While the CES has a wide-ranging agenda, its principal focus in recent times has been the operation of the BMG mine.

The locals also have had to contend with efforts by American Water Development, Inc. (AWDI) to mine the San Luis Valley's confined aquifer.[36] According to estimates from the U.S. Geological Survey, the confined aquifer is estimated to have at least two billion acre feet of water trapped in detrital sedimentary, indurated volcanic, and volcaniclastic formations at depths ranging from one thousand to over ten thousand feet below the surface of the valley.[37] This would make the San Luis Valley confined aquifer the second largest source of groundwater in the nation after the Ogallala Aquifer, which already has been extensively mined. AWDI's proposal calls for mining 200,000 acre feet of water per year from the confined aquifer.

Hypotheses

Using the above-mentioned generalizations and our understanding of the context in Costilla County, we deduced specific hypotheses that

were tested against empirical attitudinal data collected in a survey
that was part of an effort to oppose BMG operations. The data were
not collected to test hypotheses, thus the hypotheses are post-survey,
and were developed for the purpose of further examining the data.
The hypotheses are:

1) Chicanas/os in Costilla County will tend to use the local
   outdoors, such as the county park, for family activities.

2) The longer a person's residence, the less likely that person will
   be to support Battle Mountain Gold's mining operation.

3) Generally, Chicanas/os in Costilla County will oppose the
   exportation of underground water.

4) In general, the higher the proportion of Anglos in a community,
   the more support for Battle Mountain Gold's operation.

5) Chicanas/os in Costilla County will prefer agricultural and arts
   and crafts activities for economic development over mining and
   tourism-related activities.

Method

This study is based on a survey of voting-age adult residents of
Costilla County, Colorado, conducted during the summer of 1990.
Two hundred and nine (209) randomly selected residents were
interviewed for approximately five minutes each. The interview
schedule was designed to be as uncomplicated as possible by using
simple, straightforward "Yes" and "No" response categories wherever
feasible. Also, questions tended to be forced-choice (See Appendix).
Initially, interviews were conducted on a block-by-block, house-to-
house basis. Later on, interviews were conducted with residents
where they were found, such as at local churches after Sunday mass
or outside grocery stores. Interviews were conducted in both Spanish
and English, according to the preferences of the interviewees.

Results of the Survey
Sample Profile

The sample of 209 persons included both genders on a more-or- less
equally represented basis.[38] Unfortunately, because the research was
conducted with other purposes in mind (emerging as it did out of

social action concerns), the interview schedule failed to include an item on ethnicity, and thus a strict comparison between groups cannot be made. The team, however, reported that 35 (16.7 percent) of the sample were Anglo Americans and 174 (83.3 percent) were Chicanas/os. The age of respondents ranged from 18 to 91 years. The mean age of respondents was 47.5, with a mode and median of 48. The survey respondents are from all parts of Costilla County. For purposes of this study, we identified respondents according to their residence in one of ten settlements within the county.

Table 1 presents selected demographic data on the respondents. The ten residential areas include: La Corridera, Mesita, Blanca, Cuba, Ft. Garland, "Old" San Acacio, Chama, San Francisco, San Pablo, and San Luis. La Corridera is a linear strip of homesteads located between San Luis and San Pablo that is traditionally considered part of San Luis. Cuba is considered a neighborhood within San Luis proper. Approximately 48.5 percent of the respondents are residents of San Luis; 11.2 percent are from San Acacio; another 10.7 percent are from Ft. Garland; 9.5 percent are from San Pablo; 5.3 percent are from Chama; and the remainder are from San Francisco, Cuba, Blanca, Mesita, and La Corridera.

The average length of residency in the valley among respondents is approximately 41 years. The majority are life-long residents of Costilla County (67.5 percent). Another 20 percent of the respondents have lived in the county for more than 10 years. Less than three percent of the respondents have lived in the county for a period of five to 10 years; approximately six percent have lived in the county between one and five years; and less than three percent have lived in the county less than one year.

TABLE 1:
Selected Demographic Characteristics of the Respondents

Age Group	Age	
	Age Distribution	
	f	%
18-25	20	9.8 %
26-30	18	8.8
31-35	19	9.3

Table continued on next page

Table 1: (Continued)

Age Group	Age Distribution	
	f	**%**
36-40	17	8.3 %
41-45	17	8.3
46-50	24	11.8
51-55	19	9.3
56-60	20	9.8
61-65	16	7.8
66+	34	16.7 %
TOTAL	204	99.9 %**

Village of Residence***

	f	**%**
San Luis	82	48.5 %
San Pablo	16	9.5
San Francisco	5	3.0
Chama	9	5.3
San Acacio	19	11.2
Ft. Garland	18	10.7
Cuba	8	4.7
Blanca	5	3.0
Mesita	2	1.2
La Corridera	5	3.0 %
TOTAL	169	100.1 %

Length of Residence in the Valley

	f	**%**
Less than 1 year	6	2.9 %
1-5 years	13	6.2
6-10 years	6	2.9
> 10 years	43	20.6
"all my life"	141	67.5 %
TOTAL	209	100.1 %

* Missing cases = 5. Mean = 47.5. Mode = 48.0. Median = 48.0
** Percentages may not add up to 100 because of rounding.
*** Missing cases = 40.

Rito Seco County Park

Since Costilla County is the only county in Colorado without public lands, it was decided that an assessment of the use of Rito Seco County Park would provide important insights into the environmental attitudes of local residents. The park is the only facility of its kind in the entire county that is a public park in a montane ecosystem. It is located about nine miles east of San Luis in the Sangre de Cristo Mountains. The park offers opportunities for picnics, hiking, and camping, and has a source of clean spring water. The park will very likely be impacted by BMG's strip-mining and milling operations. The county road that leads to the park passes through the middle of the BMG mine site.

Table 2 presents data on the frequency and reasons for use of the county park by the respondents. Approximately 68 percent of the respondents report use of Rito Seco County Park. Nearly 32 percent of the respondents do not use the park. Respondents who use the park averaged 4.3 visits per year. Nearly 19 percent of the respondents use the park more than five times a year; approximately 17 percent use the park four to five times a year; another 15 percent use the park between two and three times a year; and nearly 17 percent use the park at least once a year. These figures indicate locals use the park regularly, with use probably being highest during the summer, as the area has fairly severe winters.

TABLE 2:
Respondents' Frequency of Use of County Park and Reasons for Use

Frequency of Use of Rito Seco County Park*		
Frequency of Use	**f**	**%**
At least once a year	35	16.9%
2-3 times a year	31	15.0
4-5 times a year	36	17.5
More than 5 times a year	39	18.9
Do not use	65	31.6%
TOTAL	206	99.9%**

Table continued on next page

TABLE 2: (Continued)

Reason for Use of Rito Seco County Park***

Reason	f	%
Family picnics	114	55.3%
Church groups	9	4.4
School groups	9	4.4
Weddings/social events	8	3.9
Hiking	36	17.5
To get spring water	27	13.1
Other	24	11.7%

*Missing cases = 3. Mean = 4.3.
**Percentages may not add up to 100 because of rounding.
***Total does not equal 100 because of multiple responses.

Local residents use the park for a variety of reasons. Over 55 percent of the respondents who use the park cited picnics with family as the primary reason for visits to the park. Nearly 18 percent use the park for hiking. Another 13 percent use the park to get spring water. Church, school, and other social groups account for about 13 percent of the use of the park.

Battle Mountain Gold Mine

Although some local leaders depict the communities of the San Luis area as bitterly divided into pro-mine and anti-mine factions, our survey results indicate that Costilla County residents are solidly united in their opposition to the BMG mining operation. Seventy-seven percent of the respondents are opposed to the mine. Only 17.6 percent support the mine, and 5.4 percent are undecided.

Opposition to the mine is not surprising. Not only are cultural orientation and values relevant, as the literature cited above indicates, but toxic problems at both national and local levels (such as the toxic spill by ESI in 1975) may have enhanced residents' sensitivities toward environmental issues and problems. Among the respondents who support the mine, and who answered the interview question dealing with reasons for support, 6.7 percent report that they support the mine because they have a job with BMG. Another 10 percent support the mine because they expect to have a job with BMG in the future.

And, finally, 83.3 percent support the mine because the people in the area need jobs. The principal reason for supporting BMG is the perceived positive impact it will have in terms of employment.

TABLE 3:
Respondents' Attitudes Toward Battle Mountain Gold by Selected Factors

Attitudes Toward Battle Mountain Gold*		
	f	%
Support mine	36	17.6 %
Don't support mine	157	77.0
Don't know	11	5.4 %
TOTAL	204	100.0 %

Reason for Support of the BMG**		
	f	%
Have a job at the mine	2	6.7 %
Expect to have a job at the mine	3	10.0
Towns need jobs	25	83.3 %
TOTAL	30	100.0 %

Reason for Opposition to BMG Mine***		
	f	%
Environmental dangers	130	66.7 %
Health hazards	97	49.5
Will hurt promotion of economic development	51	26.0
Water quality	165	81.3
Other reasons	20	10.2 %

*Missing cases = 5.
**Missing cases = 6
***Total does not equal 100.0% because of to multiple responses.

It is important to balance interpretation of these data with some qualitative impressions. On September 4, 1990, the lead author visited the mine site at the invitation of the mine operations manager. A visit with mine workers led to lengthy discussion about the mine and the environment. All eight workers present indicated they were unhappy with the impact the mine was having on the land, but lamented the fact that they had little choice but to work to put food on the table.

One worker stated: "We have never had to tear up mountains before to put food on the table. It is unfortunate that our community is forced to choose between jobs and the environment."[39] It seems clear that even workers who support the mine have ambivalent feelings about the issue: they oppose the environmental destruction, but high levels of unemployment in the county forces them to seek jobs with BMG against their better judgment.

Among those respondents who expressed opposition to the mine, 66.7 percent cited environmental threats as reasons for their views. Nearly 50 percent of those opposed to the mine cited concerns over health hazards, and 26 percent expressed concern over the effects mining may have on the promotion of economic development alternatives. Over 81 percent of the respondents believe the BMG mine will negatively impact water quality in the Rito Seco.

Table 4 presents respondents' attitudes toward BMG by village and length of residence. Although the majority of respondents opposes the establishment of the BMG mine, the survey results indicate interesting differences between villages. Persons who reside in Ft. Garland, which is located north of the mine site, are less likely than most others to express opposition to the mine. In contrast, villagers living downstream from the mine are more likely to express opposition toward BMG, suggesting that perceived direct impact might be a critical factor in engendering opposition to the mine. In San Luis, San Pablo, San Acacio, and La Corridera about four-fifths of the respondents do not support the mine. In Chama nearly three-fourths of respondents did not support the mine. In San Francisco, Cuba, and Blanca, none of the respondents favored BMG. In contrast, in Mesita and Ft. Garland the respondents were evenly split.

TABLE 4:
Respondents' Attitudes Toward Battle Mountain Gold by Village and Length of Residence

Attitudes Toward BMG by Village*				
Village	Don't Support		Support	
	f	%	f	%
San Luis	62	81.6	14	18.4 %
San Pablo	11	84.6	2	15.4

Table continued on next page

TABLE 4: (Continued)

Village	Don't Support		Support	
	f	%	f	%
San Francisco	5	100.0	0	0.0
Chama	6	75.0	2	25.0
San Acacio	13	81.3	3	18.8
Ft. Garland	9	50.0	9	50.0
Cuba	8	100.0	0	0.0
Blanca	3	100.0	0	0.0
Mesita	1	50.0	1	50.0
La Corridera	4	80.0	1	20.0 %
TOTAL N = 154	n=122		n=32	

Attitudes Toward BMG by Length of Residence**

Length of Residence:	Don't Support		Support	
	f	%	f	%
Less than 1 year	4	80.0	1	20.0 %
1-5 years	3	25.0	9	75.0
6-10 years	4	66.7	2	33.3
> than 10 years	32	88.9	4	11.1
All my life	114	85.1	20	14.9 %
TOTAL N = 193	n=157		n=36	

*Missing cases (including "Don't Knows") among those known by village = 15. Percentages are by rows.
**Missing cases (including "Don't Knows") = 16. Percentages are row percentages. Chi-square (Pearson Value) - 28.54412; 4· df; statistically significant at P = .000001.

Persons residing in Ft. Garland made up 8.6 percent of the survey participants. Of the 18 respondents from Ft. Garland, 50 percent expressed support for the BMG mine. The nine affirmative responses from Ft. Garland constitute 28.1 percent of the total number of respondents supporting the BMG mine. Although residents from Ft. Garland make up less than 10 percent of the survey participants, they are approximately 28 percent of the total number of respondents supporting the mine. The majority of residents of Ft. Garland (and Blanca) are Anglo Americans. Our survey research team noted that 20 of the 23 respondents from the Ft. Garland-Blanca area were Anglo Americans (86 percent). In contrast, less than 15 of the San Luis area respondents were noted as being of Anglo American ethnicity (about

10 percent of 144 respondents). Thus, ethnic difference may play a role in determining attitudes toward industrial mining in the San Luis Valley.

There seem to be two other reasons for the relatively lower levels of opposition to the mine among Ft. Garland residents. One is that Ft. Garland is much further removed from the mine site than are the other villages. Whereas San Luis is about three miles southwest and downstream of the mine, Ft. Garland is about seventeen miles to the north. Ft. Garland's distance from the site, and thus its relative detachment from the potential negative environmental effects of the operation, is another probable reason why its residents seem to support the mine.

Another factor is that residents of Ft. Garland use Rito Seco County Park less frequently than people from the other villages. While close to 65 percent of the total sample uses the park, only 44.4 percent of Ft. Garland respondents do so. This may mean that Ft. Garlanders have less of an interest in the condition of the park than residents of the other villages. Another, more important fact is that Ft. Garlanders will not be directly affected by mining activities. Residents of Ft. Garland do not rely on the Rito Seco for their water needs, as do the residents of the villages downstream of the Rito Seco. Therefore, if the Rito Seco is dried-out or contaminated by mining activities, the livelihoods of the residents are less likely to be impacted than those of the residents of San Luis and other downstream villages.

Support for the BMG mining operation is highest in the predominantly Anglo settlement area and lowest in the Chicana/o settlements. This, combined with the lesser likelihood of being directly impacted by the mine operation, is very likely the principal factor explaining inter-village differences in attitudes toward BMG.

Table 4 also presents data that indicate that support for BMG is related to length of residence. The percentage of respondents who support the mining operation decreases with length of residence in the San Luis Valley. Approximately 75 percent of those who have lived in the valley from one to five years support BMG. In contrast, 85 percent of those who have lived in the area their entire lives do not support the mine. Opposition to BMG increases with the length of residence. The four recent arrivals who do not support the mine may have recently left urban areas and are acutely sensitive to environmental issues.

Table 5 shows the percentage of respondents opposed to BMG by reasons for opposition, length of residence in the valley, and village of residence. Because respondents could provide multiple causes for their opposition, the figures are provided only for the major reasons given. Dangers to the environment and concern over water quality were the most often-cited reasons for opposing BMG. Among those respondents who view the mine as endangering the environment, there is a moderate relationship to length of residence in the valley, with those persons residing in the area longer being more likely to cite this concern. Except for respondents in the villages of Chama and Ft. Garland, there is a majority in each village that cites dangers to the environment as a reason for opposition to the mine. Respondents from Chama, who were the least likely to cite environmental concerns, tended to cite health hazards. Among the respondents from Ft. Garland who oppose the mine, the principal reasons for opposition are dangers to the environment and health hazards. A minority of respondents raised the issue of BMG negatively impacting alternative economic development efforts.

TABLE 5:
Percentage of Respondents Opposing BMG by Reasons for Opposition, by Length of Residence in the Valley, and Village of Residence

Dangerous to the Environment		
Length of Residence	**f**	**%**
Less than 1 year	2	66.7 %
1 to 5 years	3	100.0
6 to 10 years	4	100.0
More than 10 years	24	77.4
All my life	97	87.4 %
Village of Residence	**f**	**%**
San Luis	53	88.3 %
San Pablo	10	90.9
San Francisco	5	100.0
Chama	2	40.0
San Acacio	11	84.6
Ft. Garland	4	50.0

Table continued on next page

Table 5: (Continued)

Dangerous to the Environment

Village of Residence	f	%
Cuba	7	87.5 %
Blanca	3	100.0
Mesita	1	100.0
La Corridera	3	100.0 %

Health Hazards

Length of Residence	f	%
Less than 1 year	1	33.3 %
1 to 5 years	2	66.7
6 to 10 years	2	50.0
More than 10 years	24	77.4
All my life	68	61.3 %

Village of Residence	f	%
San Luis	44	73.3 %
San Pablo	6	54.5
San Francisco	3	60.0
Chama	5	100.0
San Acacio	8	61.5
Ft. Garland	4	50.0
Cuba	4	50.0
Blanca	3	100.0
Mesita	1	100.0
La Corridera	3	100.0 %

Will Hurt Promotion of Alternative Economic Development

Length of Residence	f	%
Less than 1 year	0	0.0 %
1 to 5 years	1	33.3
6 to 10 years	0	0.0
More than 10 years	13	41.9
All my life	37	33.3 %

Village of Residence	f	%
San Luis	23	38.3 %
San Pablo	6	54.5
San Francisco	1	20.0
Chama	1	20.0

Table continued on next page

Table 5: (Continued)

Will Hurt Promotion of Alternative Economic Development

Village of Residence	f	%
San Acacio	6	46.2 %
Ft. Garland	0	0.0
Cuba	2	25.0
Blanca	2	66.7
Mesita	0	0.0
La Corridera	0	0.0 %

Harmful to Water Quality

Length of Residence	f	%
Less than 1 year	4	100.0 %
1 to 5 years	4	36.4
6 to 10 years	4	66.7
More than 10 years	34	89.5
All my life	119	88.8 %

Village of Residence	f	%
San Luis	64	82.1 %
San Pablo	13	92.9
San Francisco	5	100.0
Chama	7	100.0
San Acacio	17	94.4
Ft. Garland	9	52.9
Cuba	7	100.0
Blanca	3	75.0
Mesita	1	50.0
La Corridera	4	100.0 %

With regard to the mine harming the water quality, which was a separate question in the interview schedule, data in Table 5 show that this perception becomes more widespread as length of residence increases. In terms of village of residence, there seems to be widespread concern about the potential harm to the water in the valley by the mining operation. In San Luis, for instance, which had the highest frequency, 82.1 percent of the respondents perceived harm to the water as a result of the mining operation. In Ft. Garland, 52.9 percent perceived harm to the water.

Water Resource Issues

The survey interview was designed to probe local views on the exportation of water from the valley to the Front Range (the plains on the eastern side of the Rockies). This issue also has generated widespread opposition among valley farmers, ranchers, and business and government leaders. We asked survey respondents if they were concerned about the exportation of water from the valley. Data presented in Table 6 indicate that more than 90 percent of the respondents are concerned about the exportation of water; 6.2 percent are not concerned, and 3.3 percent are undecided.

We also asked respondents about the likely impact the exportation of water would have on the San Luis Valley. Nearly 89 percent indicated the exportation of water would lead to the decline of agriculture in the valley. Approximately 22 percent of the respondents believe the exportation of water will lead to the loss of jobs in the valley. Further, 99 percent of the respondents believe that the exportation of water will *not* create jobs in the valley, while only one percent believe that it will create jobs.

TABLE 6:
Respondents' Attitudes Toward the Exportation of Water from the Valley

Concerned About Exportation of Water from Valley*		
Attitude	f	%
Concerned	188	90.4 %
Not concerned	13	6.2
Don't know	7	3.3
TOTAL	208	99.9 %**

Perceived Impact of Exportation of Water on Valley***		
Impact	f	%
Decline of agriculture	174	88.8 %
Loss of jobs	43	21.9
Will create jobs	2	1.0
Will not create jobs	194	99.0
Other	22	11.3 %

* Missing cases = 1.
** Total percentage does not equal 100 because of rounding.
*** Total does not equal 100 because of multiple responses.

Economic Development Issues

A final set of questions in the interview schedule dealt with the preferences of local residents toward the types of economic development in the San Luis area. Summary statistics are presented in Table 7. Ninety-seven percent of the respondents expressed support for arts and crafts as a preferred type of economic development activity; 99 percent expressed support for agricultural economic development; 91.5 percent expressed support for tourism as a viable type of economic development activity; and 99 percent expressed support for small business development. Only 19.2 percent expressed support for mining as a type of economic development activity. Opposition to mining in general was slightly greater than that expressed regarding BMG; 80.8 percent of the respondents stated that they did not support mining as a type of economic development activity. Again, the findings may be clarified in light of qualitative statements made to the research team during the interviews. Some of the respondents (n=55) expressed concerns about the role of tourism in local economic development plans. These concerns centered around the idea that "San Luis must not become another Taos."[40]

TABLE 7:
Types of Economic Development Supported by Respondents*

Type	Support		Don't Support		Total N
	f	%	f	%	
Arts/crafts	195	97.0%	6	3.0 %	201
Agriculture	201	99.0	2	1.0	203
Tourism	182	91.5	17	8.5	199
Mining	37	19.2	156	80.8	193
Small business	199	99.0	2	1.0	201

* Row percentages.

There were a variety of views regarding the dangers inherent in tourism as a strategy for economic development. What follows is a sampling of responses to the tourism question:

> If we are not careful with tourism, then too many outsiders will come here and our quality of life will be impacted.

Once outsiders come in, then we will see them buying up the land and driving our property taxes up. This is what happened in Taos; the natives will be driven out by wealthy outsiders.

I personally don't want a lot of tourists here because they can be insensitive and rude. They lack an understanding of our traditions and culture.

Tourism has the danger of destroying our cultural landscape. I don't want to see McDonald's and Burger King on our main street.

I heard some tourists from Aspen talking about how sad it is that the billionaires are driving the millionaires out of Aspen and how the millionaires will now have to move to San Luis. What will happen to our lands and homes if the wealthy move in?

Tourism is good if it is carefully regulated and controlled. We must avoid getting into a situation that places added stress on already overloaded public services.

We should not build lodging for tourists until we take care of our own needs first. We need to fix the swimming pool and deal with our sewage disposal before we start building hotels and other tourist-related facilities.

Tourism can be a very positive force for economic development, but I don't want to see our local population cleaning up toilets and garbage after the tourists.

The natural beauty of San Luis is our greatest asset. We should promote a special type of tourism, one that is sensitive to our environmental and cultural values.

While many respondents expressed similar concerns, the majority still favor tourism as an aspect of economic development. The attitudes seem to indicate strong support for tourism if it is low-impact and regulated. Local planners associated with the Economic Development Council in San Luis are cognizant of this fact as exemplified by their efforts to design development plans that are respectful of the local cultural landscape.[41]

Discussion

Studies focusing on the cultural distinctiveness of Chicanas/os in northern New Mexico and southern Colorado have found them to be emotionally attached to the land.[42] Other studies have found that

Chicanas/os in this region have serious concerns about land and water uses they perceive to be detrimental to the community and the natural environment.[43] This attitudinal survey resulted in similar findings. The findings indicate that members of the Chicana/o population in Costilla County use the local mountain park for family activities, oppose mining activities perceived as harmful to natural resources, and oppose the exportation of underground water. Chicanas/os, according to survey responses, prefer agricultural, micro-entrepreneurial, arts and crafts, and low-impact tourism activities as economic development activities that appear ecologically and culturally sustainable.

Opposition to the mine tends to be based on perceived environmental threats, such as the pollution of natural streams and potential health hazards. This finding is in sharp contrast to the view held by those mainstream environmentalists who believe that minorities are not concerned about environmental issues. Further, only a few of the respondents seemed ready to trade ecological soundness for employment. The mainstream environmentalists' view, it was found, simply does not apply to Chicanas/os in southern Colorado and northern New Mexico, where the struggle to preserve the environment occurs within cultural and psychological frameworks that place great emphasis on land. It also occurs within a historical struggle to preserve the "homeland."

Exportation of water is also opposed by locals on the basis that it will negatively impact the community by contributing to the decline of agriculture. And, although a study by Weber found that this segment of Chicanas/os are "rural landholders" rather than "farmers," since they own plots of land but do not farm them, the reasons for the lack of actual participation in agriculture are to be found in the historical patterns of economic domination of this minority group.[44] Nevertheless, there still are many successful Chicana/o farms and ranches in the area, although certainly, many others do not have sufficient capital, credit, or land to operate commercial farms.[45] Still, cultural and psychological orientations emphasize agriculture as a preferred economic activity, along with arts and crafts and limited tourism. Interestingly, Weber perceives the traditional orientation of Chicanas/os as maladaptive in a market-based economy, but completely overlooks the seeming incompatibility of a market-based economy and environmental soundness.[46] He also overlooks the fact that government officials are more interested in programs emphasizing large-scale development than in rejuvenating the local agro-ecological and subsistence systems.[47]

There is a possibility that the findings reflect urban-rural patterns rather than cultural differences between ethnic groups. For instance, some studies have found that urban persons are more concerned about the environment than those in rural areas.[48] Since Chicanas/os in the study live in the larger communities in Costilla County, this factor may be exerting an influence. However, many other studies looking for urban-rural differences have failed to find them, and we really cannot accept the view that the town of San Luis is urban.[49] It may be that occupational activity in rural areas is more important with regard to concerns about the environment. For instance, Freudenburg found that ". . .persons involved in agriculture generally prove to be *more* concerned about environmental protection than the other residents of the same communities."[50] Although many Chicanas/os in Costilla County may not be engaged in the production of agricultural commodities, they may be involved in the production of agricultural goods for household consumption. Or they may be involved in mixed production, with both limited sales of goods in local and nearby markets and simultaneous production for the home. It also may be that an agricultural orientation rather than actual production is currently salient in the case of this particular economically displaced minority segment.

Conclusions

In this study it was found that Chicanas/os in Costilla County are greatly concerned about their environment. They are opposed to mining activities that threaten local watersheds, whether they be mining operations or water exportation activities. They prefer agricultural, arts and crafts activities, small businesses, and tourism as directions for sustainable economic development in the region. All of the five hypotheses tested in this study were supported by empirical data on attitudes toward local environmental issues.

It is important to avoid stereotyping minorities as disinterested in environmental issues. It is also important to examine the salience of local environmental issues among minority populations rather than some global sense of environmental concern. Finally, some local environmental struggles must be understood within the dynamics of struggle over the "homeland."

APPENDIX

Selected Interview Schedule Items

Length of Residence	How long have you lived in Costilla County? 1) less than one year, 2) one to five years, 3) six to ten years, 4) more than ten years
Use of Rito Seco	Do you use the county park in the hills by the Rito Seco? 1) Yes, 2) No
Frequency of Use	How often do you use the county park? 1) at least once a year, 2) two to three times a year, 3) four to five times a year, 4) more than five times a year
Reason for Use	What is the main reason for going to the park? 1) picnics with family, 2) church groups, 3) school groups, 4) weddings, other social events, 5) hiking, 6) to get spring water, 9) other
Attitude Toward Mine	Do you support the establishment of the Battle Mountain Gold strip-mine? 1) Yes, 2) No
Reasons for Support	Why do you favor the mine? 1) I have a job there, 2) I expect to have a job at the mine, 3) because the town needs jobs, 9) other
Reasons for Opposition	Why are you opposed to the mine? 1) it is dangerous to the environment, 2) it is a health hazard, 3) it will hurt local efforts to promote other types of economic development, 9) other
Mine Impact on Water	Do you think the mine will affect the water quality of the Rito Seco and other creeks in the area? 1) Yes, 2) No
Exportation of Water	Are you concerned about the export of water from the valley to the Front Range? 1) Yes, 2) No

Impact of Exportation

What impact do you think the export of water will have on your community? 1) it will lead to decline of local agriculture, 2) it will not have an impact, 3) loss of jobs, 4) it will create jobs, 9) other

Economic Development

Of the following types of economic development projects, which do you support? Arts and Crafts, Agriculture (ranching and farming), Tourism, Mining, Small Business

NOTES

[1] Bullard, R., "Ecological inequities and the New South: Black communities under siege," *The Journal of Ethnic Studies* 17(4): 101-115, 1989; Day, B., and Knight, K., "The rain forest in our backyard," *Essence* January: 75-77, 93-94, 1991; Wiley, E., III, "Why people of color should think green: Scholars stress involvement in environmental movement," *Black Issues in Higher Education* 7(23): 1, 12-14, 16, 1991.

[2] Bullard, R., *Dumping in Dixie: Race, Class, and Environmental Quality* (Boulder: Westview Press, 1990); Bryant, P., "Toxics and racial justice," *Social Policy* 2(1): 48-52; 1989; Commission for Racial Justice, *Toxic Wastes and Race in the United States: A National Report on the Racial and Socioeconomic Characteristics of Communities with Hazardous Wastes Sites* (New York: United Church of Christ, 1987); Bullard, R. and Wright, B. H., "The politics of pollution: Implications for the Black community," *Phylon* 48(1): 71-78; 1986; Bullard, R., "Blacks and the environment," *Humboldt Journal of Social Relations* 14: 165-184; 1987a; Bullard, R., "Environmentalism and the politics of equity," *Mid-America Review of Sociology* 12: 21-37, 1987b.

[3] Center for Third World Organizing, *Toxics and Minority Communities*. Oakland, CA: Center for Third World Organizing, 1986.

[4] Commission for Racial Justice, *Op. cit.*

[5] Raptor Education Foundation, "Determining why minority communities demonstrate little or no interest in environmental issues." Aurora, CO: Raptor Education Foundation. Photocopied. p. 1, 1991.

[6] Hershey, M. R., and Hill, D. B., "Is pollution 'a white thing'? Racial differences in preadults' attitudes," *Public Opinion Quarterly* 41(4): 439-458, 1977-1978; Hutchinson, R., "A critique of race, ethnicity, and social class in recent leisure-

recreation research," *Journal of Leisure Research* 20: 10-30, 1988; Mitchell, R., "How 'soft,' 'deep,' or 'left'? Present constituencies in the environmental movement for certain world views," *Natural Resources Journal* 20(2): 345-358, 1980; Taylor, D. E., "Blacks and the environment: Toward an explanation of the concern and action gap between blacks and whites," *Environment and Behavior* 21(2): 175-205, 1989.

[7] Bullard, *Op. cit.*; Peña, D., "The 'Brown' and the 'Green': Chicanos and Environmental Politics in the Upper Rio Grande," *Capitalism, Nature, Socialism* 3(1): 79-103, 1992; Pulido, L., "The Los Angeles Chicano Community and Environmental Politics: What Institutional Environmentalism Can Learn from Grassroot Struggles." Research proposal submitted to the Woodrow Wilson Foundation, Rural Policy Fellowship. Graduate School of Architecture and Urban Planning, UCLA, Los Angeles, CA, 1990, and "This Land is Our Land: Nature, Natural Resources and the Struggle for Autonomous Rural Communities in Hispano New Mexico." Paper presented at the 32nd Annual Conference of the Western Social Science Association, Portland, OR, 1989.

[8] Pulido, *Op. cit.*, p. 2, 1989.

[9] Peña, *Op. cit.*, 1992.

[10] See, for example: Epstein, J., "Indigenous attempts to protect the environment: A Pacific island case," *Journal of Environmental Systems* 17(2): 131-148, 1987; Epstein, J., "Political attempts to defend the environment: A Pacific island case," *Journal of Environmental Systems* 17(3): 187-207, 1987-1988; Churchill, W., ed., *Struggle for the Land: Indigenous Resistance to Genocide, Ecocide, and Expropriation in Contemporary North America* (Monore, ME: Common Courage Press, 1993); Hecht, S. and Cockburn, A., *Fate of the Forest: Developers, Destroyers, and Defenders of the Amazon* (London: Verso Books, 1989); Peña, D., *Ibid.*

[11] Hispanics in northern New Mexico have often referred to themselves as "Spanish Americans," and sympathetic American scholars often have respected that self-referent. However, there also are other self-referents, such as *manito, paisano, taosenos,* and so on. In order to avoid confusion over these terms, we decided to refer to these peoples as a regional segment of the overall Chicana/o population.

[12] Lux, G. "Ancient aspirations: A Mexican-American view of land reform." In Geisler, C.C. and Popper, F.J., eds., *Land Reform American Style* (Totowa, NJ: Rowman and Allanheld, 1984), 188-205.

[13] Carlson, A. W., "Rural settlement patterns in the San Luis Valley: A comparative study," *The Colorado Magazine* 44(2): 111-128, 1967.

[14] Knowlton, C. S., "Land-grant problems among the state's Spanish-Americans," *New Mexico Business* 20: 1-13, 1967b; Stevens, P., "Changes in land tenure and usage among the Indians and Spanish Americans in northern New Mexico." In Knowlton, C.S., ed., *Indian and Spanish American Adjustments to Arid and Semiarid Environments* (Lubbock: Texas Technological College, 1964), 38-43.

[15] Knowlton, *Op. cit.*, 1967b; Martinez, R., "Chicano lands: Acquisition and loss," *The Wisconsin Sociologist,* 24 (2 & 3): 89-98, 1987.

[16] Rodriguez, S., "Land, water, and ethnic identity in Taos." In Briggs, C.L. and Van Ness, J.R., eds., *Land, Water, and Culture: New Perspectives on Hispanic Land Grants* (Albuquerque, NM: University of New Mexico, 1987), 313-403.

[17] Andrews, W. H., "Family composition and characteristics of an economically deprived cross cultural Rocky Mountain area," *Rocky Mountain Social Science Journal* 3(1): 122-139, 1966; Erickson, K. A., and Smith, A. W., *Atlas of Colorado.* Boulder: Colorado Associated University Press, 1985; Martinez, *Op. cit.*; McClean, R. N., and Thomson, C. A., *Spanish and Mexican in Colorado: A Survey of the Spanish Americans and Mexicans in the State of Colorado* (New York: Board of National Missions of the Presbyterian Church in the U.S.A., 1924); Sanchez, G. I., *The Forgotten People: A Study of New Mexicans.* (Albuquerque: Calvin Horn, 1940).

[18] Atencio, T. "The human dimensions in land use and land displacement in northern New Mexico villages." In Knowlton, C.S., ed., *Indian and Spanish American Adjustments to Arid and Semiarid Environments* (Lubbock: Texas Technological College, 1964), 44-52.

[19] Atencio, *Op. cit.*, p. 47. Also see Garcia, R., *A Philosopher in Aztlán: Notes Toward an Ethnophilosophy in the IndoHispano (Chicano) Southwest.* Two volumes. Unpublished doctoral dissertation. Philosophy, University of Colorado, Boulder, CO. 1988; Peña, *Op. cit.*, 1992.

[20] Knowlton, C. S., "Conflicting attitudes toward land use and land ownership in New Mexico," *Proceedings of the Southwestern Sociological Association*, 18: 60-68; p. 61, 1967a.

[21] Eastman, C., Carruthers, G., and Liefer, J. A., "Contrasting attitudes toward land in New Mexico," *New Mexico Business* 24(3): 3-20, 1971.

[22] Eastman, et al., *Op. cit.*, p. 11.

[23] Brown, F. L., and Ingram, H. M., *Water and Poverty in the Southwest.* (Tucson: University of Arizona Press, 1987).

[24] Brown and Ingram, *Op. cit.*

[25] Van Dresser, P., "The bio-economic community: Reflections on a development philosophy for a semiarid environment." In Knowlton, C.S., ed., *Indian and Spanish American Adjustments to Arid and Semiarid Environments* (Lubbock: Texas Technological College, 1964), 53-74.

[26] Van Ness, J. R., "Modernization, land tenure, and ecology: The costs of change in northern New Mexico," *Papers in Anthropology* 17(2): 168-178. p. 176; 1976.

[27] The seven counties include, in northern New Mexico, Guadalupe, San Miguel, Mora, Taos and Rio Arriba, and in southern Colorado, Costilla and Conejos.

[28] Department of Commerce, Bureau of the Census, *1990 Census of Population and Housing*, PL 94-171 Data (CDRM 451100), March 1991.

[29] See Erickson and Smith, *Op. cit.*; Ogden, J. R., and Associates. *Baca Water Project's Economic Impact on the San Luis Valley.* Alamosa: J. R. Ogden and Associates, 1989.

[30] According to Charlie Jaquez, Costilla County Committee for Environmental Soundness, in personal communication with Devon Peña, September 1990, San Luis, Colorado.

[31] Ogden and Associates, *Op. cit.*

[32] Goforth, B., *Rito Seco fish kill, Costilla County.* Colorado Division of Wildlife, Ft. Garland District. Ft. Garland: Colorado Division of Wildlife. Typewritten, 1975.

[33] Costilla County Committee for Environmental Soundness. *Chronology of BMG.* San Luis, CO: CES. Photocopied, 1989.

[34] For an in-depth analysis of the local grassroots legal and political struggles against BMG see: Peña, D. and Gallegos, J., "Nature and Chicanos in Southern Colorado." In Bullard, R., ed., *Confronting Environmental Racism: Voices From the Grassroots* (Boston: South End Press, 1993).

[35] Costilla County Committee for Environmental Soundness. *The Costilla County Committee for Environmental Soundness: Project Prospectus and Organizational Profile* (San Luis: CES. Photocopied. p. 1., 1990.

[36] See Peña, D., *Preliminary Field Report: San Luis Valley Farmer-Rancher Opposition to American Water Development, Inc..* Unpublished field report. Rio Grande Bioregions Project, Hulbert Center for Southwestern Studies, Colorado College. Photocopied. 1990.

[37] Colorado Ground-Water Association. *Water in the Valley.* (Lakewood: Colorado Ground-Water Association, 1989).

[38] The interview schedule did not include a gender identification item; however, the research team reported that about 55 percent of the respondents were female and 45 percent were male.

[39] Field interview with workers at Battle Mountain Gold mine site by Devon Peña, September 1990, San Luis, Colorado.

[40] Taos is a neighboring county south of Costilla and located in New Mexico. Its county seat, Taos, has changed demographically and culturally in dramatic fashion during the past two decades, when Anglo Americans in-migrated in relatively large numbers mainly as a result of tourism. See Martinez, R. "The rediscovery of the 'Forgotten People." In Mindiola, Tatcho, et al., eds., *In Times of Challenge: Chicanas and Chicanos in American Society* (Houston, TX: Mexican American Studies Program, University of Houston, 1988); Rodriguez, S., "Art, Tourism, and Race Relations in Taos: Toward a Sociology of the Art Colony," *Journal of Anthropological Research*, 45(1), 1989.

[41] Charles Manzanares, Economic Development Council, in personal communication with Devon Peña, September 1990, San Luis, Colorado.

[42] Atencio, *Op. cit.*; Knowlton, *Op. cit.*, 1967a.

[43] Brown and Ingram, *Op. cit.*

[44] Weber, K. R., "Necessary but insufficient: Land, water, and economic development in Hispanic southern Colorado," *The Journal of Ethnic Studies* 19(2): 127-142, 1991.

For a critique of Weber's findings see: Peña, D. and Martinez, R., *Hispanic Centennial Farms: A Cultural and Natural History of Land Ethics in Transition.* Unpublished research proposal. Hulbert Center for Southwestern Studies, Colorado College, 1993.

[45] For an agro-ecological study of commercial Chicano agriculture in the Upper Rio Grande see Peña, D., "Agroecology of a Chicano Family Farm." Paper presented at the 35th Annual Conference of the Western Social Science Association, Corpus Christi, TX. April 21-26, 1993.

[46] Weber, *Op. cit.*

[47] Van Dresser, *Op. cit.* We use the term "subsistence" with some hesitation. Further research on the agricultural history of the bioregion reveals that production for exchange has long accompanied subsistence production in Chicano family farms. See Peña and Martinez, *Op. cit.*, 1993. We would characterize the bioregional economy of the Chicana/o Upper Rio Grande as one involving "autarkic prosumption" (i.e., under favorable market conditions production goes for cash sales and under less favorable conditions the family farm produces for self-sufficient consumption; in either case, production for self-consumption remains a steady feature of the agroecological system).

[48] Freudenburg, W. R., "Rural-urban differences in environmental concern: A closer look," *Sociological Inquiry* 61(2): 167-198, 1991.

[49] Freudenburg, *Ibid.*

[50] Freudenburg, *Ibid.*, p. 193.

MEXICAN AMERICANS ON THE HOME FRONT: COMMUNITY ORGANIZATIONS IN ARIZONA DURING WORLD WAR II

Christine Marín

T he Mexican American[1] experience in Arizona during the World War II period can be studied from new perspectives and viewpoints. Other than its main importance in the social history of ethnic minorities in the Southwest, it can be placed in the context of United States social history. It can certainly be placed in the context of Mexican American, or Chicano/a history, since World War II was a major turning point for Mexican Americans.

It is generally accepted by Chicano/a historians that World War II provided a variety of opportunities for changing and improving the economic and social conditions of Mexican Americans.[2] Life outside the barrio during wartime exposed soldiers to new experiences. The G.I. Bill of Rights provided them opportunities for higher education, job training, business and home loans. Other Mexican Americans, however, continued to struggle with the common and prevalent evils of racism and discrimination in their communities. Mexican Americans were still segregated in theaters and restaurants, and barred from public swimming pools, dance halls, and other establishments. Inferior education or lack of educational opportunity for Mexican Americans remained a deep-seated problem in Arizona.

No attempt is made here to analyze the military history of Arizona's role in World War II. Instead, this essay is an attempt to explain how Mexican Americans organized themselves within their own communities to become important, patriotic contributors to the American war effort. It also shows that Mexican Americans in Phoenix and Tucson supported each other's efforts to combat racism while helping win the war for all Americans. This wartime activism was prevalent in other Mexican American communities throughout the state as well.

There are some problems, however, in writing about Mexican American participation on the home front in Arizona during the war. For example, one cannot build on previous literature, since little has been written on this topic.[3] Most Arizona historians or scholars have virtually ignored the history of Mexican Americans during this important period. In essence, they have completely failed to recognize a valid, fascinating, and viable aspect of Arizona history.[4]

Other historians, like Gerald D. Nash of New Mexico, considered the World War II period as a turning point in the Southwest. Nash believes the war transformed the American West from a "colonial economy based on the exploitation of raw materials into a diversified economy that included industrial and technological components."[5] His contention is that this changed economy encouraged the influx of larger numbers of ethnic minorities in the West, especially Mexican immigrants and African-Americans, thus diversifying the ethnic composition of the region.

Arizona was organized as a territory in 1863 and admitted to the Union as the forty-eighth state in 1912. Its population on April 1, 1940, according to the Sixteenth Census, was 499,261. Three major race classifications were distinguished in the Sixteenth Census tabulations, namely "White," "Negro," and "other races." Persons of Mexican birth or ancestry who were not American Indian or of other non-White races were classified as "White" in 1940. Thirty percent of Arizona's population was represented by persons of Mexican descent. Urban areas such as Tucson and Phoenix reflected a growing trend during this period. The urban population of Tucson in 1940 was 36,818; approximately 12,000 individuals were Mexicans and Mexican Americans. The total population of Phoenix numbered 65,414, of which roughly 15,000 were of Mexican descent.

Mexican Americans in Phoenix at this time lived in the same barrios they traditionally lived in when Anglo-American speculators, carpetbaggers, and entrepreneurs arrived in 1867. This area was near the south side of the Salt River. The land was undesirable to Anglos, mainly because of occasional heavy flooding and its proximity to unsightly railroad tracks. By 1930, the large Mexican barrio had been split into two distinct sections. The poorer district, bounded by Washington, Sixteenth, and Twenty-fourth streets and the river, contained a shack town of the poorer Mexicans, and a "7-Up Camp," a block of shacks along the north side of the railroad tracks housing hundreds of Mexican families. The second section of this same barrio was located between Second and Fourth Avenues, south of Madison Street.[7] By 1940, this same large barrio consisted of smaller barrios from within, such as "Cuatro Milpas," "Little Hollywood," and "Golden Gate." Here, Mexicans and Mexican Americans owned small businesses, stores, houses, and built and attended their own churches. They generally lived apart in poverty from the Anglo residential areas and pockets of Anglo growth and business and economic development, which were further north of the barrio. In 1941, the Phoenix Housing Authority built three separate low-income housing projects with a $1.9 million New Deal grant from the federal government. The developments were the Marcos de Niza Project for Mexicans and the Matthew Henson Project for African-Americans, both located in south Phoenix. The housing project for Anglos, named for the Phoenix flying ace of World War I fame, Frank Luke, Jr., was built in east Phoenix. These housing units were to accommodate six hundred low-income families who lived in sub-standard dwellings in the same area. Segregated housing, however, reflected the thinking of city officials and leaders who were slow to eliminate other forms of discrimination in their town.[8]

The Mexican American community of Phoenix readily supported the war effort almost immediately after war was declared late in 1941. The *Leñadores del Mundo* (Woodmen of the World), an active Mexican fraternal and life insurance society, sponsored the "Diamond Jubilee" to show Mexicano support for the war effort and for President Roosevelt. The festival and dance were held at the meeting hall of the Leñadores on the president's birthday, January 30, 1942.[9]

Other *mutualistas*, such as the *Alianza Hispano-Americana*, the *Club Latino Americana* and *La Sociedad Mutualista Porfirio Díaz* were also active in Phoenix and throughout the state during this period. The *Alianza Hispano-Americana* was a fraternal insurance society that was first organized in Tucson in 1894. Like other mutual-aid societies in Arizona, the AHA offered low-cost life insurance and social activities to its members. Mutual-aid societies provided essential support for Mexicanos in the fight against racism and discrimination. Many proved to be the sources of cultural, social, and religious cohesion in Mexicano communities.[10]

The coming of World War II saw the establishment of war-preparedness programs and training schools. The National Youth Administration (NYA) was one such New Deal program. The NYA was initiated on June 26, 1935, and provided for the educational and employment needs of America's youths. Two statewide National Defense training schools were set up under the NYA in Arizona. The training school for boys was in Tempe; the girls school was located in Coolidge. Established in Pinal County in 1926, Coolidge is approximately 30 miles south of Phoenix. Tempe, at this time, was a small farming and livestock-raising community with a population of about 3,000. It was just nine miles east of Phoenix, along the Salt River.

Tempe educators and city leaders were targets of Mexicano opposition to racism and discrimination in three separate incidents in 1912, 1925, and 1946. Mexicanos settled in what is now Tempe in 1865, when the Ft. McDowell military post was established. The early settlement of San Pablo, later known as "Mexican Town" by the Anglos of Tempe, was already firmly established in 1874. The town itself was later incorporated as "Tempe" by the Anglos in 1895. Just after Arizona statehood in 1912, Mexicanos became the center of controversy, when they learned they could not claim title to the lands which they had legally lived on and developed, because their farms and homes were in what was called "Section 16." This area, which under the new Constitution of Arizona and its precedent Organic Act, was a school section, and thus not subject to permanent settlement. Consequently, the Mexicanos lost their land.

From 1914 to 1926, only Mexican children attended the Eighth Street School. In 1915, the Tempe School District made an agreement with the Arizona State Teachers' College (now known as Arizona State University) that allowed them to use Eighth Street School as a University Training School to establish Americanization programs for the segregated Mexican children in the first through third grades. The agreement lasted until 1950-51, when the primary students moved to the nearby Wayne Ritter School. In 1925, Adolfo "Babe" Romo, whose family settled in the area in the 1800s, filed a lawsuit (now known as the "Landmark Case") on behalf of his children who were attending the segregated Eighth Street School. In October 1925, Superior Court Judge Joseph Jenckes ruled the Romo children could attend the Tenth Street Grammar School. The following Monday morning, several Mexican children attended school there. However, the enrollment at the Eighth Street School was completely Mexican American until 1945. The third racial incident involved the desegregation of Tempe Beach, the city's public swimming pool. Tempe Beach was opened in 1923, and did not admit Mexicans. It was not until 1946 that the Tempe Chamber of Commerce agreed to admit Mexican Americans to Tempe Beach in response to legal pressures from Mexican American veterans from Phoenix who formed the Tony F. Soza Thunderbird Post 41 of the American Legion.[11]

Another kind of pressure was applied to Arizona's Governor Sidney P. Osborn to integrate the training schools of the NYA in 1941. Led by Vicente Alfaro, a respected member of Tucson's Mexican American community, parents demanded that their children be allowed to participate in the NYA's resident vocational training school programs. The schools in Tempe and Coolidge provided classroom instruction to develop clerical and library skills among the girls, and enabled boys to learn and improve machine skills and welding techniques. Students also received civil defense training and learned about community safety. The training schools sought boys and girls from nearby communities, and many Mexican American youngsters from Tucson applied.

The training schools brought problems as well as opportunities to Arizona. The problems were racial, and opportunities were denied to the Mexican American youngsters. They were subjected to segregated classes and ethnic slurs. Anglo youngsters refused to interact with them, and they questioned them about their loyalties to America. The Coolidge training school director refused to accept Mexican American girls into the program because "Spanish Americans were not fit for employment in National Defense work," and felt that "it was utterly useless for them to start receiving instruction" there.[12] Alfaro wrote letters to Governor Osborn requesting that he put an end to these biased practices. He cited President Franklin D. Roosevelt's pledge to be a "good neighbor"[13] with Latin America in order to improve relations between countries as an example for Osborn to follow. In his reply to Alfaro, however, Osborn was not convinced he was the individual who could create change. Instead, Osborn reminded Alfaro that the NYA was a "federal set-up and one with which the governor, or no state official, [sic], [had] anything whatever to do. It [was] certainly under the control and management of the United States government."[14] There is nothing in the documentation to show that the matter was ever resolved. However, the Governor did ask Jane H. Rider, the Arizona administrator of the NYA, to investigate Alfaro's complaints. The record, however, is neither clear nor complete, and contains no reply to his request. Nor is there correspondence from the Governor to Vicente Alfaro regarding the incidents of racism in Tempe.[15]

Mexican American youths were targets of racism in the copper mining community of Morenci, located approximately 250 miles southeast of Phoenix. Again, the Governor's lack of action disappointed the Mexican Americans who sought his help. This time, however, several Mexicano leaders from Phoenix, who were active sponsors and organizers of the city's only Mexican American Boy Scout troop, appealed to Governor Osborn in the Spring of 1942[16] to use his power to change the long-standing segregation policy of two Morenci facilities: the Morenci Club, and the Longfellow Inn.[17]

Morenci was established as a mining camp in 1884. Bitter labor strikes and racial conflicts involving Mexicano miners and the Phelps Dodge Copper Corporation have occurred in the Clifton-Morenci mining districts since the late 1800s. Morenci is located in Greenlee County in southeastern Arizona, near the New Mexico border. The Morenci Club, owned by the Phelps Dodge Copper Corporation, offered recreational facilities to Anglos only. The Longfellow Inn was a restaurant in the community. Boy Scout Troop 134, with S.A. Morales, William R. Sanchez, S.G. Murillo, and Alberto Montoya as its leaders, planned on attending a two-day Music Clinic at the Morenci Club. Here, the group was to learn about the use of instruments and musical arrangements in the performance of musical events for their communities. Young boys and girls would sing and play patriotic music, and hear various groups perform. But their attendance and participation at the event was called off when the Scout leaders read in a local newspaper publicizing the event that "the Morenci Club and Longfellow Inn are not open to Spanish-American people." The article warned: "Please caution your students on this as we do not wish anyone to be embarrassed."[18] Outraged at such blatant and open racism aimed at the young Boy Scouts— who symbolized the youth and democracy of the United States—the scout leaders sent a signed petition to the governor so that he could respond to their concerns. In the petition they cited the humiliation, embarrassment, and shame felt by the boys in the troop. They reminded Governor Osborn that these boys were American citizens who were entitled to fair, honest, and democratic treatment in their own state. Scout leaders also asked the governor to issue an official public apology in the form of a statement in the Morenci and Phoenix newspapers in order to expose the shabby treatment of these young boys. The apology never came from Governor Osborn.[19]

Despite this racist atmosphere, other Mexican American youths in Phoenix participated in a wartime activity that involved the country at large. When the Standard Oil Company challenged all neighborhoods in July of 1942 to gather much-needed rubber for its war efforts, the youngsters from the Marcos de Niza housing project combed their Phoenix neighborhood for anything made of rubber. Gathering discarded tires and other materials, their final accumulation of rubber totalled more than 2,200 pounds, surpassing what was gathered by other youth groups in the city. Their "prize" for this accomplishment was a picnic/party, where they were treated to pies, sherbet, cakes, candy, sandwiches, and other refreshments. Rogelio Yanez, the U.S. Housing Authority's Mexican American representative for the Marcos de Niza housing project, worked with various mutualistas such as the Leñadores del Mundo, and the Alianza Hispano Americana, to sponsor and pay for the party.[20]

Other mutualistas such as the Club Latino Americana and La Sociedad Mutualista Porfirio Díaz were instrumental in organizing Mexican American cotton pickers during a drastic shortage of farm labor in the Salt River Valley's cotton fields in Phoenix. This labor shortage served as the catalyst for the Mexican American community to become united with the larger Anglo community in an emergency harvest of cotton. In October 1942 the Victory Labor Volunteers responded to the call.[21]

Long-staple cotton was desperately needed to make parachutes, blimps, and gliders for the troops overseas. These volunteer labor groups organized spontaneously and comprised members of civic clubs, women's social clubs, churches, and garden and veterans groups within the Anglo segments of Phoenix. The volunteers were headed by an informal committee whose sole interest was doing emergency war work whenever it was needed. Citizens throughout the city were encouraged to volunteer for a minimum of a half-day each week to harvest the cotton crop. They were paid three dollars per 100 pounds for long-staple cotton, and $1.50 per 100 pounds for short-staple cotton. Volunteers registered with cotton canvassers at the Phoenix Chamber of Commerce office, or at nearby U.S. Employment Service offices.[22]

The Spanish-language newspaper in Phoenix, *El Sol*, ran a lengthy advertisement in its October 9, 1942, issue calling for the Mexican American community to participate in a patriotic show of Mexicano unity and become cotton pickers.[23] Women and school children were encouraged by various mutualistas to participate in the picking and bagging of cotton, and the Phoenix Union School system permitted students to be absent from classes one day a week to do so. Transportation was provided by the city on a daily basis from various pickup locations within the Mexican American barrios of Marcos de Niza, Golden Gate, Riverside, Cuatro Milpas, and East Lake. Transportation trucks also left from neighborhood locations such as Conchos Grocery, Washington Elementary School, and the Friendly House.[24] These trucks carried Mexicanos from residential areas near Fourteenth Street and Henshaw Road; Ninth Street and Washington; and East Lake Park to the cotton fields located in the valley. It was estimated that within a three-week period, 5,000 Mexican American workers—men, women, and children—harvested over 35,000 pounds of long-staple cotton for the nation's war effort.[25] Thus, this cotton harvest emergency brought a rare opportunity for Mexicanos and Anglos to share equally in a patriotic, community effort during a tense and difficult labor and cotton shortage.

These two examples of Mexican American participation in Anglo-dominated activities may provide insight into how Mexican Americans created their own separate support systems in times of crisis, while co-existing with Anglos in meeting a larger demand. A national wartime emergency required and enabled these two groups to organize within their own communities and work together towards a larger common goal. The goal was met, even though the two groups stayed within their own social boundaries and worked separately. The tremendous responses to these critical emergencies also showed how the war briefly united Phoenicians, who crossed ethnic lines in order to meet economic challenges. In these examples, each group contributed equally to a vision of American unity and American victory, but did so separately, a point which should be emphasized.

In the early stages of the war, several military installations and air bases were established in the Phoenix area. Latino cadets undergoing training nearby were welcomed and honored by the Mexican American community with testimonial dinners, dances, social gatherings, and community meetings between February 17 and March 10, 1942.[26] These cadets came from Mexico, Brazil, Cuba, Costa Rica, Honduras, Nicaragua, and Guatemala. They symbolized Latin American friendship and support of the United States in wartime. Mexican American alumni from the Spanish Club of Phoenix Community College, "*Los Ositos*," helped in sponsoring and arranging dinners, receptions, and honoring the cadets throughout the Mexican American community.[27] The cultural ties that the community shared with these cadets reinforced feelings of ethnic and cultural pride.

Mexican Americans in Phoenix participated in other war-related community projects. American citizenship classes were taught by the bilingual staff of the Friendly House,[28] a social service center formed to provide for the needs of the Mexican and Mexican American community. Classes on the Constitution were held on a daily basis at the Friendly House, and were also available in the evening. Members of the Spanish-speaking community felt they were helping in the war effort by studying to become American citizens. Obtaining American citizenship may have been an accepted way for Mexicanos to show their patriotism and loyalty to the United States and the war effort. It was, therefore, a unique opportunity for the Mexican American community to be accepted into the larger American society that still maintained racist policies and traditions.

Mexican American boys were encouraged to become involved in Boy Scout activities. Since it was felt that the American character was formulated and developed through the scouting organization, Mexican Americans believed that their youths could be molded into productive, patriotic, and loyal Americans, eager to support their country in times of war.[29] Early enrollment numbered over 25 boys who became active in Troop 47, the only Spanish-speaking troop in Phoenix.

When the ministers of the Phoenix Ministerial Alliance of Spanish Speaking Churches met in the Mexican Presbyterian Church in February of 1943, they adopted a resolution that urged the Mexican American community to participate in war-related activities. The Alliance encouraged its members to take an active interest in city politics, and to register to vote in city elections.[30] Since the nation was at war, it was believed that Mexican Americans would become more interested in their community's political issues. Their votes would thus become a key factor in supporting the war effort abroad.

Another patriotic gesture involved public donations from the Phoenix Mexican American community in August of 1943. The editor of *El Sol*, Jesús Franco, and a prominent physician in the community, Dr. A.G. Del Valle Lugo, organized a drive to collect money for the purpose of purchasing cigars and cigarettes for American soldiers overseas, regardless of their ancestry or place of birth.

Mexican Americans took advantage of this opportunity to donate whatever amount of money they had for such tobacco purchases. Individuals were encouraged through various advertisements in *El Sol* to take their contributions to the newspaper's offices on Third Street and Washington. The patriotic fever infected the entire community. The cigarette drive began in mid-August and was scheduled to end on September 10. In spite of the wartime hardships imposed upon the community, the donations remained steady and consistent.

This patriotic gesture was lauded in issues of *El Sol* throughout the duration of the tobacco drive, and the names of those who contributed were acknowledged and printed in the newspaper. By the end of the drive in mid-September, almost $300 had been collected from the Mexican American community. Most of the donations were small.[31] The money was deposited in a local bank by the drive's treasurer, Miguel G. Robles, who later presented the money to a military representative on behalf of the Mexican American community of Phoenix. No newspaper accounts were found to indicate that the Anglo community also participated in this drive.[32]

The Mexican American community of Tucson also did its share to help win the war. Mutual-aid and benefit organizations such as the Alianza Hispano-Americana and the Leñadores del Mundo sold war bonds. Religious organizations within the Mexican Catholic parishes, such as *El Centro Club* and the *Club San Vicente* added their support by collecting scrap metal. Social and service clubs such as the *Club Latino*, *Club Treinta*, and *Club Anáhuac* also supported the Allied cause in various ways.[33] Usually, the clubs were either all male or female-male. Individual Mexican American women in Tucson also played an important part in the war effort. Through the efforts of Rose Rodriguez, a secretary at Tucson City Hall, the organization known as the *Asociación Hispano-Americana de Madres y Esposas* (the Spanish American Mothers and Wives Association) was formed in 1944.[34]

The functions of the *Asociación* were similar to those of any other patriotic organization during this period. Yet, the Mexican American women of Tucson also had some unique and distinct goals from the Anglo women who had formed their own social clubs and ladies' auxiliaries. One of their specific goals was to boost the morale of the Mexican American soldiers who were away from the Tucson area. Another goal was to build a recreation center for the exclusive use of Mexican American soldiers.

These women did not purposely segregate themselves from the other kinds of wartime activities organized by the Anglo women. Rather, they felt the need to reinforce the cultural, emotional, and traditional sentiment commonly shared among Mexican Americans whose loved ones were away at war. Through their own organization, these women sought to unite Mexicanos and Mexicanas in their community, and help them deal with the hardships caused by the war.

Women in the Asociación had sons, husbands, brothers, or other family members in the military, many of whom were serving overseas. They were young and old, and came from differing socio-economic backgrounds. Many were young homemakers, others were working-class women who toiled as section hands on the Southern Pacific Railroad. Some were secretaries or sales clerks, and still others were much older women who maintained households. Membership was not strictly limited to married women or to the mothers of servicemen. All women who wanted to participate in the group were encouraged to do so.

The early activities of the Asociación focused on the sales of war bonds and war stamps. Mexicanos and their families considered it a privilege to buy war bonds. They believed that through such sales their men serving abroad would never be without military armaments needed to defend themselves in battlefront situations.[35] In the period from April 1944 to July 1945, the association sold more than one million dollars worth of war bonds and war stamps. The purchase of these bonds and stamps were made by individuals in the Mexicano community in Tucson.

The Mexicanas of Tucson experienced war's daily trials and took on the home-front responsibilities. They collected clothing for the Red

Cross to be sent to war-torn, devastated countries. They also sent clothing to social service agencies in Mexico.[36]

The women combed their neighborhoods for scrap metal. They saved foil from candy, gum, and cigarette wrappers, and turned in large quantities of the foil to collection centers. The homemaker became just as important to the war effort as the women who worked in defense jobs. Mexicanas planted their own "victory" gardens. They learned to bottle and preserve vegetables and fruits. They saved waste fats and turned in their collections of fats and grease, which yielded glycerin for high explosives. They collected tin cans, which went into armaments and cans for the soldiers' "C" rations.

Mexicanas also maintained their household equipment in efficient shape and decreased fuel consumption. With an increasing demand for paper by the government, the supply at home was reduced. They salvaged old magazines and newspapers. They made things last, or else did without. The Asociación offered in-home child care services for mothers who were performing war-related services, such as donating blood and making bandages for the Red Cross, gathering food for the U.S.O., or performing duties required of them as air-raid wardens. Clearly, the Mexicanas proved their resourcefulness in the home.[37]

During the height of its activity, the Asociación was incorporated into a non-profit entity, and it purchased land on which to build the recreation center it so eagerly sought to erect for the Mexican American soldiers. The money to pay property taxes for the land came from the treasury and from sales of their community newspaper, the *Chatter*.[38]

By August 1945, however, many Mexican American soldiers began to return home. This signaled the steady decline of the Asociación. Some of the group's most active women soon resigned their memberships, as their families reunited. Husbands, sons, and brothers were home. With the war over, there was no longer a need for the mass distribution of the *Chatter*. There were also no more war bonds and stamps to sell at community events or gatherings.

Nevertheless some of the women kept the organization active, despite its decreasing numbers. Their goal remained the same—that of building a recreation center for Mexican American soldiers. The women also remained busy helping families adjust to postwar life.

In August 1945, the Asociación had $2,700 in its treasury.[39] While interest in the Asociación decreased in the post-war years, the activity of its leaders remained constant. Eventually, the demands of the Asociación on the few remaining members became too numerous. In 1964, twenty years after the Asociación was organized, the Arizona Corporation Commission revoked the group's non-profit certification, citing inactivity for the action. Members had at times neglected to submit annual reports. But the Asociación struggled along, continuing its effort to remain a viable and strong organization by helping the needy within their community. In 1971, they filed their reincorporation papers with the Arizona Corporation Commission with the intention of raising funds to spend on providing for the needs of the elderly. In 1976, the four remaining members of the Asociación, Lucía M. Fresno, Dolores C. Delgado, Luz M. López, and Juanita L. Loroña voted to dissolve the organization.[40]

Records do not show why the recreation center was not built after the war. It may have been too expensive to do so, or perhaps the treasury had been depleted by the property taxes the Asociación had to pay on the land it owned. Or perhaps the members no longer felt the center was necessary. The veterans were too preoccupied with finding jobs and putting their lives back together to be concerned about a recreation center. Other factors were to account for the inactivity of the Asociación over the years. As the members grew older, illness and perhaps a lack of mobility kept them from being as active in the organization. Death also took its toll on the group.[41]

In the war years, Mexicanos and Mexicanas in Arizona united their communities and committed themselves to fighting an *American* war, *their* war. And as they fought on the home front, they also struggled to retain their own unique ethnic identity. They strengthened the cultural bonds among themselves in order to reaffirm their own brand of American identity.

Mexican Americans in Phoenix and Tucson needed their own heroes and heroines who could personalize and simplify the larger wartime struggle. The Mexican Americans in these communities proved themselves to be such homefront heroes and heroines, meeting the challenge to advance the Allied cause, while retaining the morale of their communities through social and cultural activities.

In spite of the culture clashes with Anglos, and the prevalent racism and prejudice against them, the Mexican Americans shared with the larger society the intent to win the war abroad. Unfortunately, however, this shared goal of victory during wartime was not enough to break all the existing racist barriers. The Mexican American soldiers fighting overseas for democracy left behind those in their hometowns to struggle for this same goal in Arizona. Mexican men, women, and youths in Phoenix and Tucson created their own separate American home front activities in their own communities. They left behind a legacy which is manifested in a cultural and ethnic pride that can be defined simply as "Mexican Americanism."

This form of nationalism, pride in one's ethnicity and cultural history, coupled with the patriotism of Mexican Americans, convinced many of them that racism was un-American and unpatriotic. These individuals took on the responsibility of eradicating it from this country.

The Mexican American soldier was the cultural and historical symbol of Americanism and social equality. At home, the Mexican Americans were the brave patriots who remained loyal to America as they sacrificed their loved ones for freedom and democracy. Such a sacrifice is the legacy the Mexican Americans of the 1940s leave behind for the rest of us to acknowledge and remember.

NOTES

[1] The term "Mexican American," as used in this paper, literally means a combination of both Mexican and American. I use it in a generic sense to include *Mexicanos*, *Latinos*, Spanish-Americans and the *Hispanos* who lived in the southwestern states of Arizona, California, New Mexico, Texas, and Colorado. I may use the terms interchangeably in order to reflect the terminology used during the World War II period in the Southwest. Mexican Americans also used these terms interchangeably to identify themselves, and the terms are found throughout Spanish-language newspapers during this period. The terms group together those who speak Spanish, and imply a cultural, linguistic, and social bond which unites the Spanish-speaking in the Southwest.

[2] The role of the Mexican American in World War II in Chicano/a history has been interpreted by Rodolfo Acuña, *Occupied America: A History of Chicanos,* 2nd edition, (New York: Harper & Row, 1981); Ralph C. Guzmán, "The Political Socialization of the Mexican American People," (Ph.D. diss., University of California, Los Angeles, 1970); Carey McWilliams, *North From Mexico: The Spanish-Speaking*

People of the United States (New York: Greenwood Press, 1968); Matt S. Meier and Feliciano Rivera, *The Chicanos: A History of Mexican Americans* (New York: Hill and Wang, 1972); Robin Fitzgerald Scott, "The Mexican-American in the Los Angeles Area, 1920-1950: From Acquiescence to Activity," (Ph.D diss., University of Southern California, 1971). The work by Raul Morin, *Among the Valiant: Mexican-Americans in WW II and Korea* (Alhambra, Calif.: Borden Publishing Co., 1966) stands out as the definitive work which cites the military participation and outstanding heroism of the Mexican American soldier on the battlefront. Mario T. García expertly defines and examines the rise of the Mexican American generation in Los Angeles in his article, "Americans All: the Mexican American Generation and the Politics of Wartime Los Angeles, 1941-45," *Social Science Quarterly*, Vol. 65, No. 2 (June, 1984), 278-289; Christine Marín, "Chicanos in World War II Phoenix" (Paper presented at the National Association of Chicano Studies 10th Annual Conference, Arizona State University, Tempe, AZ, 25-27 March 1982).

[3] Contributions made by Mexican American women in Tucson have been documented in: Christine Marín, "La Asociación Hispano-Americana de Madres y Esposas: Tucson's Mexican American Women in World War II," *Renato Rosaldo Lecture Series Monograph*. Vol. 1, (Tucson: Mexican American Studies & Research Center, The University of Arizona, 1985), 5-18.

[4] Harry T. Getty, *Interethnic Relationships in the Community of Tucson* (New York: Arno Press, 1976) provides a social analysis of Tucson's Mexican American community during the period between 1945 and 1947. The prominent Spanish-language newspapers of Phoenix and Tucson, *El Sol* and *El Tucsonense*, should be considered primary sources of vital information on the wartime activities of Mexican Americans.

[5] Gerald D. Nash, *The American West Transformed: The Impact of the Second World War* (Bloomington: Indiana University Press, 1985), vii.

[6] U.S. Bureau of the Census. Sixteenth Census of the United States: 1940. *Population. Second Series. Characteristics of Population. Arizona.* (Wash., D.C.: USGPO, 1941), 3; 36; Nash, *The American West Transformed*, 110.

[7] Michael J. Kotlanger, "Phoenix, Arizona: 1920-1940," (Ph.D. diss., Arizona State University, Tempe, 1983), 427-428.

[8] It is common knowledge that racism and discrimination towards ethnic and racial minorities prior to and during World War II was prevalent in Phoenix. See: Michael J. Kotlanger, "Phoenix, Arizona: 1920-1940," (Ph.D. diss., Arizona State University, Tempe, 1983); Herbert B. Peterson, "A Twentieth Century Journey to Cíbola: Tragedy of the 'Bracero' in Maricopa County, Arizona, 1917-1921," (Master's thesis, Arizona State University, 1975); Christine Marín, "Patriotism Abroad and Repression at Home: Mexican Americans in World War II." Unpublished Manuscript, 1977; James E. Officer, "Arizona's Hispanic Perspective" 38th Arizona Town Hall, May 17-20, 1981 (Phoenix: Arizona Academy, 1981); Bradford Luckingham, "Urban Development in Arizona: The Rise of Phoenix," *Journal of Arizona History*, Vol. 22, No. 2, (Summer, 1981), 197-234; Shirley J. Roberts, "Minority Group Poverty in Phoenix," *Journal of Arizona History*, Vol. 14, No. 4, (Winter, 1973), 347-362.

See also the newspaper articles: "¡Que Hay Discriminación y Segregación de los Mexicanos en Arizona!," *El Sol*, 4 Feb. 1943; "Hay Escandalosa DISCRIMINACIÓN: Valientemente se enfrenta a ésta situación el Diputado Francisco Robles y J.C. Carreon," *El Sol*, 11 Feb. 1943; "Perdónalos Señor," [Editorial] *El Sol*, 18 Feb. 1943; "Advertancias acerca de la discriminación," *El Sol*, 13 March 1942; "Discriminación Mexicana en Phoenix," *El Sol*, 18 June 1943; "Afrentosa discriminación en Phoenix," *El Sol*, 2 July 1943; "Phoenix will rot . . . unless it integrates, says a controversial report," *New Times* (Phoenix), 19-25 Dec. 1984; "Racial ban common in deeds in Valley, attorney maintains," *Arizona Republic* (Phoenix) 1 Aug. 1986, sec. A.

[9] "Grandioso Baile," *El Sol*, 23 Jan. 1942.

[10] See: Kaye Lynn Briegel, "Alianza Hispano-Americana, 1894-1965: A Mexican American Fraternal Insurance Society," (Ph.D. diss., University of Southern California, 1974); James D. McBride, "Liga Protectora Latina: An Arizona Mexican-American Benevolent Society," *Journal of the West*, Vol. 14, No. 4, (October, 1975), 82-90; James E. Officer, "Sodalities and Systemic Linkage: The Joining Habits of Urban Mexican-Americans," (Ph.D. diss., University of Arizona, 1964); José Amaro Hernandez, "The Political Development of Mutual Aid Societies in the Mexican American Community: Ideals and Principals," (Ph.D. diss., University of California at Riverside, 1979). See also the newspaper accounts: "Resurgiran los Latinos," *El Sol*, 3 April 1942; "Los Mexicanos en Esfuerzo de Guerra," *El Sol*, 16 Oct. 1942.

[11] *Governor's Files: George Wiley Paul Hunt*. Box 3. File Folder #29: "Schools, Segregation in." Arizona Department of Library Archives and Public Records. Phoenix, Arizona; Ruby Haigler, "Tempe, the Center of the Garden Spot of Arizona." Unpublished Manuscript, 1914. Arizona Collection. Hayden Library. Arizona State University, p. 7; "Historical and Architectural Survey. Prepared for the City of Tempe Neighborhood Development Program." Vol. 1. Prepared by a Joint Venture, CNWC Architects and Gerald A. Doyle & Associates. Unpublished Manuscript. 1976. Arizona Historical Foundation. Hayden Library. Arizona State University, p. 19; "Obituary: Rose Frank," *Tempe Daily News*, 8 Feb. 1985, *Tempe School District No. 3. Centennial History*. (Tempe: Tempe Elementary School District, 1977), 1; Rodolfo Acuña, *Occupied America: A History of Chicanos*. 2nd edition (New York: Harper & Row, 1981), 330.

[12] See the correspondence from Vicente Alfaro to Governor Osborn, July 31, 1941, and August 8, 1941, in: *Governor's Files: Sidney Preston Osborn. Listing 1940-1946*. Box 19: "National Youth Administration for Arizona, 1940-1942." Arizona Department of Library, Archives and Public Records. Phoenix, Arizona.

[13] In his 1933 inaugural address, Franklin D. Roosevelt pledged to be a "good neighbor" to Latin America in order to improve diplomatic relations. This approach improved hemispheric relations and paved the way for cooperation and security during World War II. See: Edward O. Guerrant, *Roosevelt's Good Neighbor Policy*. (Albuquerque: University of New Mexico Press, 1950).

[14] *Governor's Files: Sidney Preston Osborn. Listing. 1940-1946*. Box 19: "National Youth Administration for Arizona, 1940-1942. Arizona Department of Library, Archives and Public Records, Phoenix, Arizona.

[15] *Ibid.* Osborn letter to Jane Rider, August 8, 1941.

[16] *Governor's Files: Sidney Preston Osborn. Listing. 1940-1946.* Box 20: "Race Prejudice, 1941-1942." Arizona Department of Library, Archives and Public Records. Phoenix, Arizona.

[17] See Joseph F. Park, "The History of Mexican Labor in Arizona During the Territorial Period," (Master's thesis, The University of Arizona, 1961); Roberta Watt, "History of Morenci, Arizona," (Master's thesis, The University of Arizona, 1956); Michael E. Casillas, "Mexicans, Labor, and Strife in Arizona, 1896-1917," (Master's thesis, University of New Mexico, Albuquerque, New Mexico, 1979), 82-105; James Ward Byrkit, "Life and Labor in Arizona, 1901-1921: With Particular Reference to the Deportations of 1917," Ph.D. diss., Claremont Graduate School, 1972; James R. Kluger, *The Clifton-Morenci Strike: Labor Difficulty in Arizona, 1915-1916* (Tucson: The University of Arizona Press, 1970); A. Blake Brophy, *Foundlings on the Frontier; Racial and Religious Conflict in Arizona Territory* (Tucson: University of Arizona Press, 1972); James B. Allen, *The Company Town in the American West* (Norman: University of Oklahoma Press, 1966), 43-49, 103.

[18] *Governor's Files: Sidney Preston Osborn. Listing. 1940-1946.* Box 20: "Race Prejudice, 1941-1942." Arizona Department of Library, Archives and Public Records. Phoenix, Arizona.

[19] *Ibid.*

[20] "Los niños Mexicanos de Phoenix triunfaron en el certamen de hule," *El Sol,* 4 July 1942.

[21] For lengthy accounts of the achievements by the Mexican American "Victory Labor Volunteers," see the following newspaper articles: "Los Mexicanos en Esfuerzo de Guerra," *El Sol,* 16 October 1942; "Constituye un Mayúsculo Mérito para los Mexicanos que se han sumado a los Voluntarios de la Victoria," *El Sol,* 23 October 1942; and "La Pizca del algodón," *El Sol,* 30 October 1942.

[22] See the newspaper accounts: "Canvassers to seek cotton field army," *Arizona Republic,* 28 September 1942; "Labor Volunteers reach 3,476 total," *Arizona Republic,* 30 September 1942; "Arizona cotton-picking project needs 2,500 more workers," *Arizona Republic,* 3 October 1942; "Victory labor drive sparks city's greatest community effort," *Arizona Republic,* 4 October 1942.

[23] "Muy Importante," [Advertisement], *El Sol,* 9 October 1942.

[24] The Friendly House was one of the agencies that grew out of the Americanization Movement. It was founded in 1921 through the efforts of the Phoenix Americanization Committee. Plácida García Smith, a former teacher from Conejos, Colorado, and director of the Friendly House from 1931 through 1963, was active in the Mexicano community and became dedicated to helping in the Americanization of Mexican immigrants in Phoenix. For an excellent account of the Friendly House and the Americanization Movement in Phoenix, see: Mary Ruth Titcomb, "Americanization and Mexicans in the Southwest: A History of Phoenix's Friendly House, 1920-1983" (Master's thesis, University of California at Santa Barbara, 1984).

[25] See: "La Pizca del algodón," *El Sol*, 30 October 1942 and "Victory Labor drive sparks city's greatest community effort," *Arizona Republic*, 4 October 1942.

[26] See the following: "Bolitín de la Comunidad Marcos de Niza," *El Sol*, 17 February 1942; "En la comunidad Marcos de Niza," *El Sol*, 20 February 1942; "Homenaje a los Cadetes Latinos," *El Sol*, 23 February 1942.

[27] "El Junior College festeja a los cadetes Hispano-Americanos," *El Sol*, 10 March 1942.

[28] "Se darán clases de Constitución," *El Sol*, 4 February 1943.

[29] "Boy Scouts, Tropa 47 del Corazón de María," *El Sol*, 11 February 1943.

[30] "Vote is urged by ministers," *Arizona Republic*, 23 February 1943.

[31] For various accounts of this cigarette drive, see the following articles: "¡Para Los Soldados!," *El Sol*, 20 August 1943; "Se formaliza la campaña de colección de fondos para envio de cigarros a los soldados," *El Sol*, 27 August 1943; "La Colecta para cigarros," *El Sol*, 10 September 1943; "¡Nuestra colecta para los cigarros!," *El Sol*, 1 October 1943.

[32] "¡Para los Soldados!," *El Sol*, 20 August 1943.

[33] For a social analysis of the Mexican American community in Tucson, Arizona, between 1945 and 1947, see Harry T. Getty, *Interethnic Relationships in the Community of Tucson*. The newspaper, *El Tucsonense*, is a major primary source of important information that reveals much about the wartime activities and concerns of the Mexican American community. See also Chapter 14, "Mexicans in Tucson on the Eve of World War II," in Thomas E. Sheridan's *Los Tucsonenses: The Mexican Community in Tucson, 1854-1941* (Tucson: The University of Arizona Press, 1986), 235-248.

[34] See: Christine Marín, "La Asociación Hispano-Americana de Madres y Esposas," 5-18.

[35] Rose Rodríguez Caballero, interview with author, Tucson, 18 January 1985.

[36] *Chatter.* (Tucson). 20 August 1944.

[37] Rose Rodríguez Caballero, interview with author, Tucson, 18 January 1985.

[38] "Old 'Little Cart' Lives On," *Arizona Daily Star*, 24 June 1976, sec. C.

[39] *Chatter.* (Tucson). 17 August 1945.

[40] "Old 'Little Cart' Lives On," *Arizona Daily Star*, 24 June 1976, sec. C; Rose Rodríguez Caballero, interview with author, Tucson, 18 January 1985.

[41] Some of the information used in this history of the *Asociación* has been published. See: Christine Marín, "La Asociación Hispano-Americana de Madres y Esposas," 5-18.

MEXICAN AMERICAN CATHOLICISM IN THE SOUTHWEST: THE TRANSFORMATION OF A POPULAR RELIGION

Alberto L. Pulido

Introduction

This essay is part of a larger research project that seeks to understand symbols as sources of power and empowerment for powerless and disenfranchised communities. It focuses primarily on religious symbolism representative of the Mexican American Roman Catholic community in the United States. The study suggests that such symbols are part of a larger economic, political, ethnic, linguistic and social reality that can serve to form and mobilize such communities. Past research by the author has established that religious symbols, beliefs and practices, and, in a larger sense, the interpretation of what is considered sacred, emerge out of specific racial/ethnic traditions. These traditions represent the source of intergroup conflict, as diverse groups mobilize to control symbolic resources, and mold "official" religious symbols, representative of religious institutions.[1]

The purpose of this research is to trace the history of such conflict between Mexican American Catholics and the dominant Catholic hierarchy, and to assess its impact on Mexican American religiosity in the American Southwest. It is assumed that Mexican American Catholicism is molded and structured by history, and is best understood through an interpretive historical sociological analysis.[2] Mexican American religious symbolism, it is argued, is best described as "non-official" or "popular" religiosity[3] that originated from within the laity, separate from the hierarchy of the Roman Catholic Church, and remains outside the structures of institutional Catholicism. The marginalization of this religious form has been accentuated ever since the United States' occupation of the Southwest and the formal establishment of the American Catholic Church. In sum, the marginalization of Mexican American Catholicism in contemporary society is the outcome of historical processes and relationships. What follows is a discussion of this transformation in Texas and New Mexico.

Transformation of Mexican Catholicism

The end of the Mexican-American War in 1848 brought with it major changes to Mexican Catholicism in what had been Mexico's northern frontier. Prior to the war, Mexican Catholicism was preserved by a popular and informal base, and reproduced without the imprint of the official Catholic hierarchy. For example, as early as the 18th century, *Los Hermanos Penitentes* (Confraternity of Our Father, Jesus the Nazarene) were vital for the maintenance of community unity in Northern New Mexico. They flourished in the early 19th century as a result of spiritual neglect by Catholic clergy.[4] As a mutual-aid society, they functioned as a civil and ecclesiastical organization, leading the community in prayer, worship, and catechism. At the same time, they made sure everyone had the basics for a decent quality of life through collective irrigation and the harvesting of the lands.[5] *La Hermandad* included an official *rezador* (prayer leader), and *cantor*, who led in song and public prayer at rosaries and wakes. They spiritually consoled and offered material aid for the dying and their families. This form of popular religion expressed the lifestyle, beliefs, and values that were interwoven with Mexican culture throughout the northern frontier. It was largely created in a Catholic atmosphere that lacked the presence of a religious clergy.

With the establishment of the American Catholic Church after 1848, this type of "self-reliant" religion[6] was transformed from a popular to a marginal and deviant religious tradition, because ecclesiastical authority was now controlled and structured by a new European clergy. Whereas Mexican religiosity and the Spanish language were once considered normative dimensions of Catholicism along the northern frontier, they were now replaced by new languages and traditions in the new American Southwest. Traditional Mexican *peregrinaciones* (pilgrimages) and special religious days were forgotten or terminated and replaced with French, and later, Irish canons of institutional Catholicism. This new official Catholicism, imported by a foreign clergy, disrupted a "way of life" in Mexican communities at both civil and religious levels throughout the Southwest. We turn first to an examination of Texas.

Texas

The French clergy was instrumental in restructuring the Catholic Church in South Texas. After the official signing of the Treaty of Velasco, declaring Texas independent from Mexico, the Republic of Texas was established in August of 1836. To determine if the ecclesiastical administration should remain in the hands of the Mexicans, the Prefect of the Sacred Congregation of Cardinals de Propaganda Fide, empowered Bishop Antonio Blanc of New Orleans to send delegates to inspect Texas in January of 1838. Father John Timon, rector and president of St. Mary of the Barrens College, along with a Spanish priest, were ordered on March 30 to go to Texas on a special ecclesiastical visit.[7]

Having visited only two Texas municipalities, Timon received word from San Antonian representatives (an area he had been dissuaded to visit) that religious instruction had been absent from their city for years. These representatives signed sworn affidavits about the laxity and religious neglect of Fathers Refugio de la Garza and José Antonio Valdez, priests at the Church of San Fernando.[8] It was stated that these two prelates did not hear confessions, did not distribute communion, and did not attend to the dying. Timon referred to them as "two plagues who were destroying the region with their scandalous behavior," even though he had never met them.[9]

On July 18, 1840, the Republic of Texas was granted official recognition by the Vatican. Rome designated it a prefecture of the New Orleans diocese, with Father John Timon as its Prefect Apostolic of Texas. Bestowed with the power to act as bishop, he appointed Father Jean Marie Odin from New Orleans as his Vice-Prefect Apostolic.[10] Soon after arriving in San Antonio in July of 1840, Odin decided to exercise his newly acquired power. On August 6, 1840, Odin's first official act as Vice-Prefect Apostolic was to remove de la Garza as pastor of San Fernando. Four days later he defrocked José Antonio Valdez.[11]

The arrival of a European clergy in South Texas began to transform the "normative" religious structures as perceived by the Mexican/ Mexican American community. Certain Oblate priests assigned to the

Texas valley harbored strong anti-Mexican sentiments that typified ethnocentric and racist views of the time. Father Florent Vanden-berghe, a Frenchman who became Superior of the Oblate priests in 1874, for example, felt repugnance towards his new assignment. He would have preferred to receive a mission "amongst civilized people" in Northern Texas, or in Louisiana if the opportunity arose.[12] A more blatant hatred was expressed by Dominic Manucy, a clergyman of Italian and Spanish descent who, in 1874, was named Apostolic Vicar of Brownsville, Texas. Manucy made the following comment regarding his recent appointment:

> I consider this appointment of Apostolic Vicar of Brownsville the worst sentence that could be given me for any crime. . .In the Brownsville district. . .the Catholics are exclusively greaser-Mexican-hunters and thieves. You cannot obtain money from these people, not even to bury their parents. . . .[13]

Manucy's perception of the "cheap" Mexican would remain with him throughout his tenure in the Valley of Texas[14] and serve to rationalize the new "judgement" rendered upon Mexican Catholics by the French hierarchy.

Yet, as the institution sought to control and eventually routinize the sacred, the Mexican American community embraced a religiosity interlaced with their everyday life. Hence, popular religion played an important role in sustaining Mexican Catholics in South Texas, functioning as a strategy to cope with a foreign hierarchy that sought to discredit their religious world-view.[15] It gave Mexicans a nominal allegiance to the new American Catholicism, and simultaneously provided them with the ". . .psychic margin to circumvent the proscriptions of institutional Catholicism."[16] Furthermore, popular religion provided a sense of order and stability in an otherwise chaotic and senseless world. It also gave a voice to a unique type of Catholicism, set apart from the controls of the Catholic hierarchy. According to historian Arnoldo De León:

> Autonomy rendered them the sense of security and strength to control their own privacy and reaffirm their cultural uniqueness and differences from Anglo Americans. Thus, religion was no small part of a cultural makeup that defined their identity as Texans.[17]

As in the Mexican Independence period, non-official dimensions of Mexican Catholicism were maintained because of a lack of native clergy.[18] However, this time it was a French hierarchy that did not understand the importance of the native clergy to Mexican American communities in South Texas. For example, during the 1850s Bishop Odin chose to bring in Oblate priests from Canada for his diocese, instead of attempting to create a native clergy. Throughout the unstable history of the various seminaries in the Galveston dioceses, there appeared only one individual of Mexican descent who reached the novitiate, brother José Marie García. Unfortunately, García died of yellow fever in 1858.[19]

In summary, the Mexican religious experience in South Texas is characterized by beliefs and practices that were maintained and survived outside the institutional Catholic context. The Mexican Catholic laity constructed places for prayer close to the community. The use of *altarcitos*, (religious altars), and home devotions were common practices to keep the spirit of religion alive among a community without a clergy.[20] It was the job of parents and grandparents to inculcate and provide religious instruction to their children and grandchildren.[21] José Roberto Juárez provides an interesting example of a self-described hierophant who guided the Mexican community in Sunday prayer, and presided in funeral services during the 1830s in Nacogdoches. On *días de fiesta*, this individual draped himself in an alb and chasuble and recreated his version of the mass in neighborhood *jacales* (modest homes).[22]

It is important to underscore that the relationship between the French clergy and the Mexican laity was not always antagonistic. There exist historical examples of the clergy's support of Mexican religious practices in Texas.[23] However, history reveals that the French hierarchy made no attempt to understand and build its institution on the traditions initiated by Mexican Catholicism in Texas.[24] As the new institution of American Catholicism began to unfold in the American Southwest, Mexican Catholics found their "community of memory"[25] ignored, and absent from the institutional vision of the American Catholic Church.

New Mexico

The history of Mexican Catholicism in New Mexico is one of an ethnic community which is deeply rooted in its Indo-Hispano-Mexican religious traditions. As discussed above, religious traditions such as those of Los Hermanos Penitentes, firmly established their roots in Northern New Mexico. However, unlike the *Tejanos*, New Mexicans had adopted a strong religious identity and received dynamic leadership from a native clergy that included Padre Antonio José Martínez and Padre Mariano de Jesús Lucero. But with the arrival of French clergy after the Mexican-American War, New Mexican Catholics found themselves challenged and confronted by an insensitive, ethnocentric clergy led by Jean Baptiste Lamy.

On July 19, 1850, the Holy See of the Roman Catholic Church acted favorably on a request from the VII Council of Baltimore, and established the New Mexican Territory, which included present-day Arizona and Southern Colorado as a vicariate. Jean Baptiste Lamy, a recently ordained priest from France, was named Vicar Apostolic *"in partibus infidelium"* ("in the region of the infidels"), and sent from the Ohio Valley to take over the Santa Fe diocese. Within a short period, conflict erupted between Lamy and the native clergy. By the end of the conflict, five native priests were expelled by Lamy, the most famous being Padre Antonio José Martínez of Taos.

Padre Martínez is a major figure in New Mexican history. He was the scholastic father for native clergy, and highly influential among the citizenry of Taos. His life encompassed three distinct epochs of Mexican history. He was born on January 17, 1793, in Abiquiu when New Mexican property was under the control of the Spanish Crown. In 1822, Antonio Martínez was ordained a priest, one year after Mexican independence. The ideals of liberation offered by Mexico's first revolutionary hero, Padre José Miguel Hidalgo y Costilla, deeply influenced the life of Padre Martínez, and his views on civil and ecclesiastical authority.[26]

In 1826, Padre Martínez was assigned the pastorship of Nuestra Señora de Guadalupe in Taos, New Mexico. Soon after, he created schools for children at the Indian pueblos, and the nearby Hispano villages. By 1834, Padre Martínez had established a "preparatory seminary" out of which 16 native priests were ordained. In 1835, he began to publish books and newspapers with the first manual press (*imprenta manualita*) west of the Mississippi.[27] In 1846, Padre Martínez, now 53, experienced the cession of New Mexico to the United States. Conflict between the native priest and the new French bishop ensued, and the accomplishments of Padre Martínez were soon forgotten.

On January 1, 1853, Bishop Lamy wrote his first pastoral letter to the laity. It introduced new rules for re-instituting tithing, something banned in Mexico by the Law of San Felipe in 1833. Lamy ordered sanctions for those who did not comply. The pastoral letter stated:

> . . .if anyone persisted in ignoring the obligation he would 'with great pain and regret' deny him the sacraments and such a person would be considered outside the fold.[28]

From Lamy's perspective, a good flock was one that remained ". . . devoted to right order and legitimate authority,"[29] and hence, the mark of a "successful" church was one that adopted the official practice of tithing.

However, for Padre Martínez, tithing was considered a burden for the laity. He had consistently opposed inflexible taxation because of the burden it placed on the poor.[30] As a young priest, he was at the forefront of abolishing church tithing imposed by Mexican civil law in 1833.[31] In a local newspaper, Padre Martínez expressed his opposition to Lamy's recently imposed sanctions. For Bishop Lamy, Martínez's actions were interpreted as a boycott to force him out of the diocese.

Lamy retaliated with a more severe church policy. In a second pastoral letter issued on January 14, 1854, Bishop Lamy incorporated church dogma on the Immaculate Conception to underscore the importance of tithes and the consequences for those who failed to comply:

> Any family which does not fulfill the fifth precept of the Church (to support the church materially) will not have the right to receive the holy sacraments. Let us again inform you that we consider those as not belonging to the Church who do not observe this precept; and we like-wise would take away all faculties to say Mass and administer the sacraments from all pastors who fail to sustain and provide for the maintenance of religion and its ministers. . . .[32]

Church fees related to services provided by the church were as follows: marriages, eight dollars; burials, six dollars; burial of a child under seven years of age, two dollars; and baptisms, one dollar. The bishop did allow for "those of meager resources" to pay only one-half of these fees.[33] Such church fees were a major burden for a community dependent on a barter economy. A wage economy did not exist in the area until the 1870s, when the railroad arrived in Southern Colorado.[34]

On May 5, 1856, a Basque priest by the name of Damasio Taladrid was named to replace Padre Martínez, who had written to Lamy indicating his desire to retire. Unfortunately, the relationship between Talidrid and Martínez proved confrontational. On July 23, 1856, Taladrid reported to Lamy that Padre Martínez was working on an article for the *Gaceta,* a local newspaper, and was often seen together with his friend Padre Lucero of Arroyo Hondo. When an article calling for the abolition of tithes appeared in the *Gaceta* on September 3, Padre Lucero was suspended by Bishop Lamy on the grounds that he had close associations with Martínez.[35]

On October 23, Taladrid informed Bishop Lamy that Martínez was celebrating Mass in his private oratory, and was taking over some parish functions. The following day Lamy suspended Padre Martínez. Lamy deprived him of canonical faculties because Martínez had celebrated Mass in the oratory. His suspension would remain in effect until he retracted his article from the *Gaceta.*

As a person who had studied canon and civil law extensively, Martínez protested these actions. On November 12, 1856, he wrote to Lamy, arguing at length that his suspension was null and void as prescribed by canon law. He stated that his publication of letters on the matter of tithes were protected by guarantees of "republican free speech." He stated:

> I beg your excellency to respect my viewpoint for what I am about to say. . .The diocesan statutes invite the faithful to enter into mercantile agreements making the parish priests appear like hucksters or traders. They also make the sacraments, Masses, and other spiritual gifts as so much merchandise in a warehouse by order of Your Excellency. . .Compare this way of acting with the account of Simon Magus in the Acts of the Apostles. . .[36]

This, plus five additional pleas, were ignored by Lamy. In June of 1857, formal excommunication procedures against Padre Martínez were set in motion. A native Mexican priest, Eulogio Ortiz was sent to Taos to replace Taladrid.[37] Within five months, Padre Antonio José Martínez was formally excommunicated by the Santa Fe diocese.

The salient issue in the Lamy-Martínez conflict revolves around differences in religious expression and interpretation. History reveals that Lamy was prejudiced and biased against New Mexican Catholicism prior to setting foot on New Mexican soil.[38] In 1851, en route to New Mexico from Ohio, Lamy traveled by way of New Orleans and Galveston. French bishop Jean Marie Odin, head of the Galveston Vicariate, did not hesitate to offer his interpretation of the native people and clergy of New Mexico.

He warned Lamy that it would be a mistake to go to Santa Fe without the support of six to a dozen zealous and entirely devoted newly imported priests.[39] According to Odin, Lamy would encounter:

> . . .Scandalous native clergy, and a public, especially among the Anglo Americans, who were waiting for reforms with the arrival of the new bishop. What could Lamy do alone and without support? If he should have occasion to banish a recalcitrant priest, without having someone to replace him, might not the people protest and perhaps insist on keeping the excommunicated priest in defiance of their bishop?[40]

Bishop Odin continued to counsel Lamy, advising him to go immediately to France, instead of New Mexico, and recruit a number of priests. While in France, he could better prepare himself in the Spanish language, and procure new vestments to replace the old rubbish he would encounter in all the New Mexican churches.[41]

Even though Lamy proceeded with his travel west, it is clear that Odin biased Lamy, who had not set eyes on the people of New Mexico. Recall that Odin's first assignment as Vice-Prefect Apostolic of Texas was to remove the two remaining Mexican priests. By 1868, Lamy boasted in letters back to his home province of Auvergne, that he had created a "little Auvergne" in New Mexico. By this date, Lamy's two assistants and three fourths of his priests were natives of Auvergne.[42]

As an area with deeply rooted religious traditions, New Mexico presents a history of conflict between a native and foreign clergy that adversely affected the native people of New Mexico. Unlike Texas, New Mexico had a firmly established religious community with leaders who challenged and confronted the new religious system imposed upon them by a European clergy. However, like their Texan counterparts, Mexican Catholics in New Mexico found themselves marginalized and segmented from the new American Church. The Penitentes, for example, maintained the stronghold of traditional Mexican Catholicism in Northern New Mexico during the 19th century. As one who clearly disapproved of Penitente religious practices, Lamy sought to control and redefine their traditions. Lamy instituted the practice of verification before administering the sacraments in order to stop Penitentes from receiving communion unless they renounced their membership in the brotherhood.[43] La Hermandad was driven into a position of protest and self-defense that profoundly affected their collective expressions as a civil and ecclesiastical organization.[44]

Analysis

The transformation of Mexican American Catholicism in the American Southwest is best understood from a historical and sociological perspective that is sensitive to the popular, non-official elements of Mexican American religiosity. What emerges is a self-reliant religious tradition, representative of an integrative world-view of a specific ethnic group, which, with the incorporation of the American Southwest, comes into conflict with a "legitimate," and ethnically-distinct clergy. Mexican American Catholics become unorthodox Catholics, ". . .uninstructed in the faith and deficient in their adherence to the general norms of church practices,"[45] transforming their religion from a popular to a marginal tradition. Accordingly, a historical analysis establishes the patterns and structures of Mexican American Catholicism by which its sociological significance can be interpreted.

For example, the transformation of Mexican Catholicism in the history of the American Southwest helps address the "problems" of leadership formation and collective action in the Mexican American community. The change, from a popular to a marginal belief system, has brought forth a group of believers who have few, if any, leadership roles within the American Catholic Church. For the most part, they have remained inactive within the formal structures of the institution because of the neglect and misunderstanding of the hierarchy.[46] Whereas other disenfranchised groups like African Americans have developed social movements and leaders through their religious structures and traditions,[47] Mexican American Catholics have been discouraged from taking an active leadership role in their church and community. In fact, there are numerous examples in the history of the Chicano Movement where the American Catholic hierarchy has been diametrically opposed to collective action for economic and political change in the Mexican American community. Consider that the Roman Catholic hierarchy did not collectively support César Chávez and the United Farm Workers until eight years into the movement. This despite the fact that official Roman Catholic teachings in the *Rerum Novarum* supported a workers right to unionize in the 19th century. In 1973, the National Conference of Catholic Bishops presented a farm labor resolution stating their support for free and secret ballot elections.[48]

On the other hand, what becomes very apparent in examining the history of Mexican and Mexican American religiosity in the Southwest, are the collective forces at work in its popular, non-official beliefs and practices. Mexican American popular religion emerges out of an economic, political, linguistic, and cultural reality that is representative of the everyday life experiences of a people. Hence, in the history of Mexican Americans, popular religion has functioned to establish and provide community, and create collective action as people coalesce around religious symbols that possess no institutional imprint. Throughout history, the American Catholic hierarchy has not recognized this important contribution.

From a methodological standpoint, more historical research is needed to capture the informal structure provided by popular religion utilized by Mexican Americans and other disenfranchised groups in the United States.[49] The religious symbols, beliefs and practices used by powerless communities to mobilize change need to be documented. Additional research, for example, on the histories of the Black church, ghost dance religions, and popular religious expressions in the United Farm Workers movement, is needed to identify the empowering elements of religion for these groups.[50] Yet such an approach cannot rely solely on secondary documents. Rather, it requires a methodological approach that will incorporate primary historical documents and oral histories in order to discover the actual experiences of Mexican and Mexican American religiosity. Feminist scholarship, for example, has enhanced our understanding of the Latina religious experience from this perspective.[51] Since Mexican religiosity originated outside the canons of Roman Catholicism, one need not begin an analysis from a structural perspective, but instead, from the everyday life experiences of the community. This will help us rediscover and validate the Mexican American religious experience.

NOTES

[1] Alberto L. Pulido, "Mexicanos and Religion: Understanding Ethnic Relations in the American Catholic Church." Paper presented at the National Association for Ethnic Studies, California State Polytechnic University, March 8, 1991; Alberto L. Pulido, "Race Relations in the American Catholic Church: An Historical and Sociological Analysis of Mexican American Catholics," (Ph.D. diss., University of Notre Dame,1989), 153-56.

[2] Mexican American Catholicism is described as ". . .an active process, incorporating relationships that are constantly changing through time." E.P. Thompson, *The Making of the English Working Class* (New York: Vintage, 1963), 9; Also see: Theda Skocpol, "Emerging Agendas and Recurrent Strategies in Historical Sociology," in *Vision and Method in Historical Sociology*, ed. Theda Skocpol (Cambridge: Cambridge University Press, 1984), 368-69.

[3] Popular religion or *religiosidad popular*, is a racial or ethnic group's collective interpretation of the sacred. It is an integrative world-view that includes all dimensions of life: magical, symbolic, imaginative, mystical, farcical, theatrical, political, and communal. Ricardo Ramirez, C.S.B., *Faith Expressions of Hispanics in the Southwest* (San Antonio: Mexican American Cultural Center, 1990), 6-7.

[4] David J. Weber, *The Mexican Frontier 1821-1846: The American Southwest Under Mexico* (Albuquerque: University of New Mexico Press, 1982), 79. *La Hermandad* is a lay brotherhood introduced into New Mexico from Southern Mexico or Guatemala, during the 18th century. Unfortunately, much that has been written on the brotherhood focuses on its annual practice of corporal penance. Francis Leon Swadesh, *Los Primeros Pobladores: Hispanic Americans of the Ute Frontier* (Notre Dame: Notre Dame Press, 1974), 74-5; Fray Angelico Chávez, *But Time and Chance: The Story of Padre Martinez of Taos, 1793-1867* (Santa Fe: Sunstone, 1981), 47; Also see: Marta Weigle, *Brothers of Light, Brothers of Blood: The Penitentes of the Southwest* (Santa Fe: Ancient City Press, 1976); José A. Hernandez, *Mutual Aid for Survival: The Case of the Mexican American* (Malabar: Robert E. Krieger, 1983), Chapter 1; Paul Kutsche and Dennis Gallegos, "Community

Functions of the Confradía de Nuestro Jesús Nazareno," in *The Survival of the Spanish American Villages*, ed. Paul Kutsche (Colorado Springs: The Research Committee, 1979), 91-98; Luciano C. Hendren,"Daily Life on the Frontier," in *Fronteras: A History of the Latin American Church in the USA Since 1513*, ed. Moises Sandoval (San Antonio: Mexican American Cultural Center, 1983), 133-37

[5] Hendren, 134; Barnabas C. Diekemper, "The Catholic Church in the Shadows: The Southwestern United States During the Mexican Period," *Journal of the American West*, Vol. XXIV, No. 2 (April 1985): 46-55.

[6] Moises Sandoval, *On the Move: A History of the Hispanic Church in the United States* (New York: Orbis, 1990), 21-2.

[7] José Roberto Juárez, "La Iglesia Católica y el Chicano en Sud Texas: 1836-1911," *Aztlán*, Vol. 4, No.2 (Fall 1974), 219. Note: Father Timon did not begin his journey until January 2, 1839.

[8] It is important to note that these San Antonian representatives were two men who did not have the *tejano*'s best interest in mind when describing the Mexicans of this region. The representatives were Juan Seguin and José Antonio Navarro. There was political tension between de la Garza, Seguin, and Navarro, since Padre De la Garza was a delegate to the state legislature and the national congress. He was labeled a "political enemy" by Seguin and Navarro. Juárez, 219-220.

[9] Juárez, 219.

[10] Ricardo Santos, "The Age of Turmoil," in *Fronteras: A History of the Latin American Church in the USA since 1513*, ed. M. Sandoval (San Antonio: Mexican American Cultural Center, 1983), 161.

[11] Santos, 161-62. On July 16, 1841, Pope Gregory XVI named John Marie Odin bishop of the Vicariate Apostolic of Texas, and on March 6, 1842, Odin was consecrated Bishop of Texas, severing all ties with Mexico and the Diocese of Nuevo León.

[12] Juárez, 227-29.

[13] Juárez, 229.

[14] Juárez, 234-41.

[15] Coping strategies are a response to structurally imposed demands placed upon individuals or groups. The goal is to develop active strategies that attempt to alter or restructure these demands. See: Algea D. Harrison and Joanne H. Minor, "Inter-role Conflict: Coping Strategies and Satisfaction Among Black Working Wives," *Journal of Marriage and the Family* 40 (November 1978): 183-206.

[16] Arnoldo De León, *The Tejano Community 1836-1900* (Albuquerque: University of New Mexico Press, 1982), 138.

[17] De León, 153.

[18] Mexican independence brought about a sharp decline in Spanish religious clergy along the Mexican frontier. According to the Ministro de Justicia y Negocios Eclesiasticos, there were 4,229 clerics in 1810, compared to only 2,282 by 1831. According to Santos, the decline in clergy is attributed to the following: 1) 200

priests were said to have been executed by the Spanish royalists during the course of the war, 2) 300 Spanish-born priests returned to Spain, and 3) the remaining 1,447 were said to have died of "various causes." Santos, 159. By 1828, nearly half of the frontier parishes lacked resident priests, only a limited number of clergy were scattered throughout the northern frontier by 1846. There were no priests in present-day Arizona, five in Alta California, and a total of eleven priests in New Mexico. These parishes were considered undesirable by priests due to the isolation, hardship, danger, and low salaries. Additional factors include: 1) the competition with other careers for young Mexican men, 2) lack of Mexican bishops to ordain new priests, and 3) lack of religious institutions to provide seminary training. Weber, 71-74; Also see: Juan Romero, *Reluctant Dawn: Historia Del Padre A.J. Martinez, Cura De Taos* (San Antonio: Mexican American Cultural Center, 1976), 11. In addition, prelates were also scarce along the northern frontier. Neither Mexican Catholics in Texas or Arizona saw a bishop set foot in their regions throughout the entire Mexican period of the Southwest, reinforcing the emergence of popular religiosity in the Mexican Catholic community. Weber, 71-74.

[19] Juárez, 223-24.

[20] Diekemper, 48. See: Mary Xavier Holyworthy, *Father Jaillet: Saddlebag Priest of the Nueces* (Austin: Von Boekmann-Jones 1948), 45-48, for examples from the Fort Stockton and Fort Davis regions.

[21] Diekemper, 48.

[22] This nameless person stepped-in as religious leader when the local priest, Fray Jóse Antonio Díaz de León was killed in a skirmish near Big Sandy Creek on November 4, 1834. Juárez describes this Mexican layman as an "alcoholic beadle" who performed a "parody" of the Catholic mass. Juárez, 219.

[23] For example, Jean Marie Odin was supportive and impressed with the 1841 Our Lady of Guadalupe celebration in San Antonio, Texas. He had "...seen few processions more edifying." Timothy M. Matovina, "Our Lady of Guadalupe Celebrations in San Antonio, Texas, 1840-1841," *Journal of U.S. Hispanic/Latino Theology*, (forthcoming), 1.

[24] This is due to the following: 1) The French clergy did not understand Mexican Catholicism, and 2) The strong anti-Mexican sentiments held by Anglos impacted tremendously on the views of the clergy. With Roman Catholics representing the minority in Texas, the French clergy had to pledge their allegiance to this newly acquired American territory, and therefore, could not embrace the Mexican world-view. In addition, they had to look to the Anglo as their new neophyte who now controlled the economic and political arenas of this new society. Juárez, 220-22, 245.

[25] A community of memory is one that does not forget its past. It is involved in retelling its story, and in so doing, offers examples of the men and women who have embodied and exemplified the meaning of real community. This is an important function of the religious experience in the Mexican American commu-

nity. See: Robert Bellah, Richard Madsen, William M. Sullivan, Ann Swidler, and Steven M. Tipton, *Habits of the Heart: Individualism and Commitment in American Life* (New York: Harper and Row, 1985), 153.

[26] Romero, *Reluctant Dawn,* 7; Chávez, 23-24.

[27] Chávez, 43-50.

[28] Romero, 28.

[29] Romero, 2.

[30] Romero, 2.

[31] Romero, 2. Note: New Mexicans, in general, were opposed to tithing on practical grounds that had little to do with the spiritual authority of the church. They argued that these monies only served to enrich the collectors, and claimed that the money did not remain in the province. Weber, 75.

[32] Romero, 29.

[33] Hendren, 202.

[34] Sarah Deutsch, *No Separate Refuge: Culture, Class, and Gender on an Anglo-Hispanic Frontier in the American Southwest: 1880-1940* (New York: Oxford).

[35] Romero, 30.

[36] Romero, 31-32.

[37] Although Padre Ortiz was the younger brother of Padre Martínez' dear friend, the Vicar Juan Felipe, the duties of Padre Ortiz involved an implementation of diocesan tithing policies. Romero, 33.

[38] In particular, see the work of Fray Angelico Chávez, 1981; and Fray Angelico Chávez, *Tres Macho-He Said: Padre Gallegos of Albuquerque, New Mexico's First Congressman* (Santa Fe: William Gannon,1985). Both works offer a revisionist interpretation of New Mexican Catholic history.

[39] Paul Horgan, *Lamy of Santa Fe* (New York: Farrar, Straus and Giroux, 1975), 92.

[40] Horgan, 92.

[41] Horgan, 92.

[42] Hendren, 197.

[43] Swadesh, 76.

[44] Hernandez, 21.

[45] Patrick McNamara, "Dynamics of the Catholic Church," in *The Mexican American People,* ed. Leo Grebler, et al. (New York: Free Press, 1970), 449.

[46] Alberto L. Pulido, "The Religious Dimension of Mexican Americans" in *A History of the Mexican American People,* eds. Julian Samora and Patricia Vandel Simon (Notre Dame: Notre Dame Press, 1993), 223-34.

[47] Aldon D. Morris offers an excellent description of Black religious traditions and their relation to social movements in *The Origins of the Civil Rights Movement: Black Communities Organizing for Change* (New York: Free Press, 1984).

[48] See Alberto L. Pulido, "Are You an Emissary of Jesus Christ?: Justice, the Catholic Church and the Chicano Movement." in *Explorations in Ethnic Studies,* Vol.14 (January, 1991), 17-34.

[49] Existing research reveals that the religious behavior of ethnic minorities is clearly distinct from the established patterns of institutional religion. Bradford P. Kenny, Ronald E. Cromwell, C. Edwin Vaughan, "Identifying the Socio-Contextual Forms of Religiosity Among Urban Minority Group Members," *Journal for the Scientific Study of Religion* 16 (1977), 237-44.

[50] Numerous scholars have implemented this perspective when discussing the dynamics of communities and nations in the Third World. See: Emile Sahliyeh, *Religious Resurgence and Politics in the Contemporary World* (Albany: University of New York Press, 1990).

[51] See: Gloria Inés Loya, P.B.V.M., "The Hispanic Woman: Pasionaria and Pastora of the Hispanic Community," in *Frontiers of Hispanic Theology in the United States,* ed. Allan Figueroa Deck, S.J. (Maryknoll: Orbis, 1992); Susana L. Gallardo, "A Church of Their Own: Chicana/Mexicana Catholics in San Jose." Paper Presented at XXI Annual National Association for Chicano Studies, March 24-27, 1993, San Jose, California. The ground-breaking work on what has come to be known as "Mujerista Theology" is Ada María Isasi-Díaz and Yolanda Tarango, *Hispanic Women: Prophetic Voice in the Church* (San Francisco: Harper and Row, 1988).